PERFORMANCE EVALUATION OF HEDGE FUNDS

Edited by Greg N. Gregoriou, Fabrice Rouah, and Komlan Sedzro

BeardBooks
Washington, D.C.

Library of Congress Cataloging-in-Publication Data

Performance evaluation of hedge funds / edited by Greg N.
Gregoriou, Fabrice Rouah, and Komlan Sedzro.
p. cm.
Includes bibliographical references and index.
ISBN 1-58798-199-8 (softcover)
1. Hedge funds. I. Gregoriou, Greg N., 1956- II. Rouah, Fabrice, 1964- III. Sedzro, Komlan, 1964-

HG4530.P425 2003
332.63'27--dc21
2003052184

Printed in the United States of America

PERFORMANCE EVALUATION OF HEDGE FUNDS

TABLE OF CONTENTS

PREFACE

The idea for this book came about when we realized that a collection of articles dealing with quantitative and qualitative analyses of hedge funds could be a useful addition to current existing books on the subject. These articles are meant to introduce readers to some of the issues faced by academics and practitioners working with hedge funds. They deal with current methods of hedge fund tracking and evaluation that we believe are vital for proper selection and monitoring of these funds. Although many of the articles are technical in nature, with econometric and statistical modeling often employed, emphasis has been put on interpretation and applicability of the results rather than on their theoretical development. We feel this book can help guide institutional investors, pension fund managers, endowments, and high net-worth individuals wishing to monitor the performance of hedge funds and other alternative investments.

Greg N. Gregoriou
Fabrice Rouah
Komlan Sedzro

ACKNOWLEDGMENTS

We have many colleagues to thank for their helpful comments, suggestions, and guidance during the course of writing the articles that constitute this book. First and foremost we thank Mr. Richard E. Oberuc, Sr., at LaPorte Asset Allocation System (www.laportesoft.com) for providing data on hedge funds, as well as Mr. Sol Waksman of The Barclay Group (www.barclaygrp.com) for providing data on commodities trade advisors.

We extend special thanks to Professors Carol Alexander, Paul Allison, Tim Anderson, Masoud Asgharian, Bud Bowlin, B. Wade Brorsen, Jean Brunel, Gordon deBrouwer, Fernando Diz, Laurent Favre, Wayne Ferson, Keith Hollingsworth, Alexander Ineichen, Tarja Joro, Harry Kat, Mario Lavallee, François-Serge LHabitant, Thomas Schneeweis, William F. Sharpe, Emmanuel Thanassoulis and Joe Zhu. We also thank Mr. David Dow at www.alternativesoft.com as well as Mr. Matthew Jones and Jenny Brightman at www.banxia.com for database and software support. We also thank Ms. Noelle Schultz for revision of the manuscript.

We are especially grateful to Ms. Susan Marshall and Professor Stephen Satchell, both at Henry Stewart Publications, London, England (www.henrystewart.com) and to Ms. Allison Adams and Mr. Harry Katz, both at Institutional Investor (www.iijournals.com) for permission to reproduce the following articles:

On the Market Timing Ability of Hedge Fund Managers (*Journal of Wealth Management*)

Performance Evaluation of Funds of Hedge Funds Managers Using Conditional Alphas and Betas (*Derivatives Use, Trading and Regulation*)

Fund of Hedge Fund Performance Appraisal Using Data Envelopment Analysis (*Journal of Wealth Management*)

Performance of the Ten Largest CTAs in Extreme Market Events and S&P 500 Months (*Journal of Pensions Management*)

Performance of the Twenty Largest Funds of Hedge Funds (*Journal of Pensions Management*)

Do Stock Market Indices Move The Ten Largest Hedge Funds? A Cointegration Approach (*Journal of Alternative Investments*)

Nonstationarity Tests of Managed Futures (*Journal of Wealth Management*)

Do Hedge Fund Returns Follow Random Walks? (*Derivatives Use, Trading and Regulation*)

Last Year's Winning Hedge Fund as This Year's Selection: A Simple Trading Strategy (*Derivatives Use, Trading and Regulation*)
Large Versus Small Hedge Funds: Does Size Affect Performance? (*Journal of Alternative Investments*)

Pitfalls to Avoid when Constructing a Fund of Hedge Funds (*Derivatives Use, Trading and Regulation*)

The Role of Hedge Funds in Pension Fund Portfolios: Buying Protection in Bear Markets *(Journal of Pensions Management)*

Hedge Fund Survival Lifetimes (*Journal of Asset Management*)

ABOUT THE EDITORS

Greg N. Gregoriou is visiting assistant professor of finance and research coordinator in the School in Business and Economics at the State University of New York (SUNY, Plattsburgh). He has authored over 30 articles on hedge funds, managed futures, and CTAs in various U.S. and U.K. peer-reviewed publications. He is also hedge fund editor for the Derivatives Use, Trading and Regulation a peer-reviewed journal published by Henry Stewart Publications in London, England. He was also awarded best paper prize with Fabrice Rouah and Robert Auger at the Administrative Sciences Association of Canada (ASAC) Conference in London, Ontario in May 2001. He also has over 20 professional publications in brokerage and pension fund magazines. He currently provides hedge fund and CTA quantitative and qualitative research for a large Canadian corporation and specializes in the construction and monitoring of funds of hedge funds using advanced statistical techniques with Fabrice Rouah.

Fabrice Rouah is Institut de Finance Mathématique de Montréal (IFM2) Scholar, and Ph.D. Candidate in Finance, McGill University, Montreal, Quebec. Mr. Rouah is a former Faculty Lecturer and Consulting Statistician in the Department of Mathematics and Statistics at McGill University. He specializes on the statistical and stochastic modeling of hedge funds, managed futures, and CTAs, and is a regular contributor in peer-reviewed academic publications on alternative investments.

Komlan Sedzro is Professor of Finance, and Director, Applied Master's Program in Finance, University of Quebec at Montreal. He obtained his Ph.D. in 1992 from Laval University, and since then has published many peer-reviewed articles on banking, hedge funds, and managed futures. Dr. Sedzro is also an advisor to the Montreal Derivatives Exchange.

CHAPTER 1

INTRODUCTION TO HEDGE FUNDS

BRIEF HISTORY

The first hedge fund was first created in 1949 and was set up as a private investment partnership by Alfred Winslow Jones, who hedged the risk of his fund by purchasing undervalued stocks and shorting overvalued ones. His idea of a Market Neutral fund was one in which gains and losses were eliminated from market movements, thus "hedging" the fund against market fluctuations. Using variants of his new dynamic strategy, all the while monitoring changing conditions in the market, Jones was able to outperform the average equity mutual fund (Caldwell and Kirkpatrick (1995); Chadha and Jansen (1998)). The use of leverage was also a key element of Jones' strategy, and is still used by hedge fund managers worldwide. Hedge funds are loosely regulated and generate profits by exploiting price inefficiencies and market trends in global financial markets. Professor Stephen Brown of NYU defines them as simply "funds with no rules."

Since 1949, the number of hedge funds and assets under management has grown substantially, with a sharp increase during the 1990s. Increasing volatility in world financial markets and frequent devaluations of currencies have caused huge amounts of capital to shift into hedge funds. When used properly, hedge funds are a valuable risk management tool, because they can protect an investment portfolio against cyclical pressures and unforeseen events (Jorion (2000)). It is now common knowledge that including hedge funds will enhance diversification and increase risk-adjusted performance, mainly because of their low correlation to equity, bond, and currency markets (Table 1.1). For further reading on the history of hedge funds, readers are referred to Lederman and Klein (1995), or Temple (2001).

Table 1.1.
Correlation of Returns
Zurich Capital Markets Database, 1990 to 2001

Strategy	*Market Neutral*	*Long*	*Event driven*	*Short*	*Global macro*	*Global int'l*	*Global emerging*	*Global established*	*Sector*	*Fund of funds*	*S&P 500*	*MSCI World index*
Market Neutral	1.00											
Long	0.71	1.00										
Event driven	0.66	0.72	1.00									
Short	–0.46	–0.85	–0.66	1.00								
Global macro	0.54	0.58	0.51	–0.42	1.00							
Global int'l	0.62	0.60	0.70	–0.53	0.51	1.00						
Global Emerging	0.40	0.59	0.48	–0.44	0.28	0.53	1.00					
Global established	0.68	0.88	0.78	–0.86	0.55	0.69	0.49	1.00				
Sector	0.55	0.82	0.67	–0.80	0.50	0.54	0.42	0.83	1.00			
Fund of funds	0.75	0.72	0.73	–0.65	0.70	0.79	0.55	0.81	0.71	1.00		
S&P 500 Index	0.46	0.76	0.58	–0.72	0.40	0.48	0.44	0.80	0.65	0.35	1.00	
MSCI World index	0.45	0.75	0.51	–0.69	0.31	0.49	0.50	0.74	0.58	0.31	0.84	1.00
Bond index	0.18	0.01	0.07	–0.01	0.17	–0.03	–0.02	0.10	0.11	0.02	0.20	0.15

Source: Zurich Capital Markets (ZCM) / LaPorte Allocation System

Figure 1.1
Stress Testing: August 1998 Second Worst S&P 500 Month since 1960

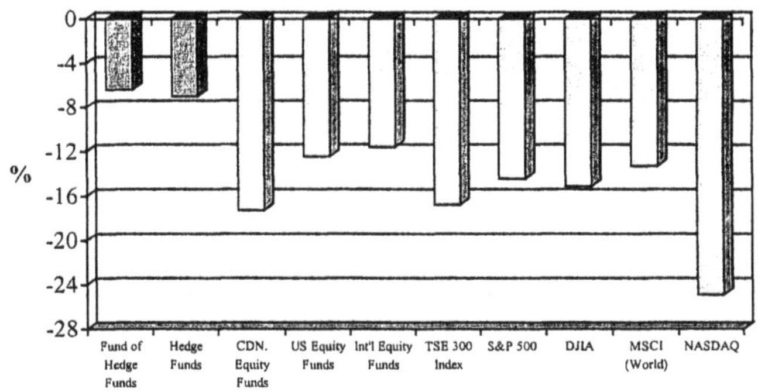

Source: Managed Accounts Report MAR/LaPorte

Well-publicized controversies such as George Soros' speculative attack on the British pound in 1992, and the collapse of Long-Term Capital Management (LTCM) in 1998, have brought notoriety to the hedge fund industry. While these and other events have received extensive coverage in professional journals and the mainstream press, the coverage in academic journals is in its growth stage. Furthermore, global macro hedge funds have often come under criticism by the media because of their large bets on macroeconomic trends or on currencies. However, during the Russian ruble crisis of August 1998, hedge funds fared better than the S&P 500 Index (August 1998 was the second worst S&P 500 month since 1960), the Morgan Stanley Capital International World Index (MSCI World), and most equity mutual funds (Figure 1.1). The performance of hedge funds during this crisis was not properly acknowledged in the press. In contrast, the meltdown of LTCM was front-page news (Edwards (1999)).

FEATURES OF HEDGE FUNDS

Hedge funds are privately pooled investments, usually structured as a partnership between the fund manager and the investors. They are not permitted to advertise and U.S.-based funds are not bound by regulation from the Investment Company Act (1940). Approximately 50 percent of hedge funds are domiciled in offshore jurisdictions, while most of the rest are based in Europe or the United States, with most hedge fund managers located in New York City.

Onshore hedge funds are only loosely regulated and subject to certain restrictions, the most notable being a maximum of 499 qualified investors. They are not required to disclose performance information to the Securities and Exchange Commission (SEC) or other regulatory offices, but many choose to report this information to specialized database vendors.

Offshore funds do not pay capital gains taxes and are subject to less regulation from home governments, and will therefore trade more frequently than onshore hedge funds. Once an onshore hedge fund reaches its limit of 499 investors, a mirror fund is often set up offshore to accommodate the new entrants.

Unlike conventional funds that track indices or adopt particular investment styles, such as growth, value, income or mid-cap, hedge funds are designed for minimum exposure to market movements. Typical investors into hedge funds are high net-worth individuals and institutional investors such as foundations, life insurance companies, endowments, and investment banks. Today, U.S. (onshore) hedge funds are limited to accredited investors with a net worth exceeding $1 million, but a fund of hedge funds (a basket of hedge funds) allows more modest investors to enter this exclusive world of privately managed money.

Hedge funds are useful because they provide liquidity in global stock, bond, and currency markets. They focus on absolute returns in all market conditions, rather than matching benchmark returns, such as mutual funds, inasmuch as to offer higher risk-adjusted returns than mutual funds and stock market indices (Figure 1.2). Hedge funds are becoming an important avenue for investors opting to diversify their traditional portfolios and better control risk.

HEDGE FUNDS VERSUS MUTUAL FUNDS

Contrary to the buy and hold strategies employed by mutual funds, hedge funds use dynamic strategies along with investments positions that are sometimes highly leveraged. Unfortunately, this makes hedge funds notorious as speculating vehicles. The investment strategies adopted by hedge funds are designed to generate absolute returns in all market conditions and they are generally less sensitive to market movements than mutual funds. Hedge funds offer attractive risk/return characteristics (Figure 1.3) as well as protection during negative S&P 500 quarters. As well, the risk-adjusted performance of most hedge fund styles is superior to that of traditional stock and bond market indices (Table 1.2). Indeed, the volatility of hedge funds is closer to that of bonds than mutual funds or equities (Figure 1.4).

Figure 1.2
Annualized Risk Adjusted Returns 1990-2001
Hedge Funds, Funds of Hedge Funds, Mutual Funds and Market Indices

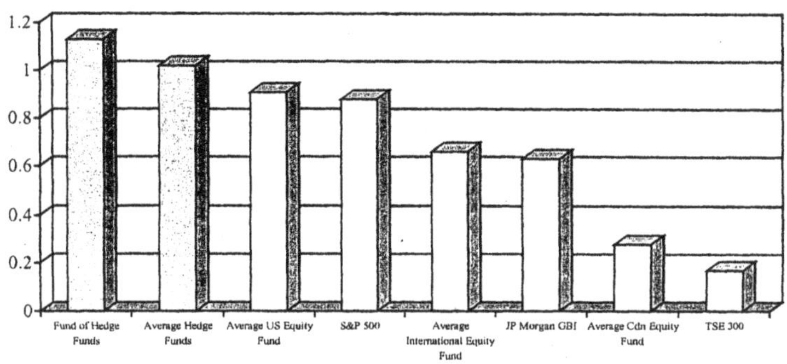

Source: MAR/LaPorte

Figure 1.3
Risk and Return Tradeoff: 1990-2000

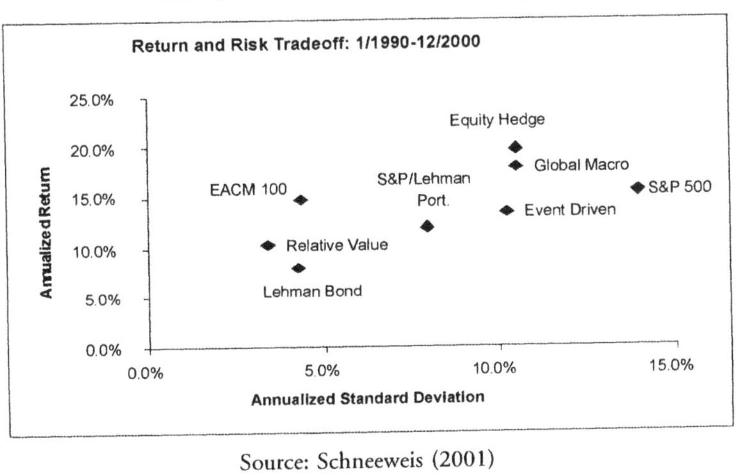

Source: Schneeweis (2001)

Table 1.2
Hedge Fund Performance, 1990-2001

	Annualized Measures			
Strategy	*Average return (%)*	*Standard deviation (%)*	*Sharpe ratio*	*Comounded return (%)*
Market Neutral	14.23	3.22	3.10	443
Long	16.42	20.66	0.59	281
Event driven	15.31	6.36	1.74	506
Short	6.47	19.54	0.11	73
Global macro	16.68	9.40	1.33	594
Global international	14.9	8.63	1.24	469
Global emerging	25.8	25.33	0.85	1,381
Global established	19.5	10.46	1.46	859
Sector	26.2	15.92	1.38	1,835
Fund of funds	11.65	5.63	1.32	295
S&P 500 index	13.21	14.55	0.62	327
World index	7.84	14.59	0.25	125
Bond index	7.71	4.24	0.82	149

Source: ZCM/LaPorte. The long and sector categories begin in August 1992; the world index is the Morgan Stanley Capital International Index and the bond index is the Salomon Brothers Aggregate Bond Index in USD.

Figure 1.4 Annual Standard Deviation of Hedge Funds, Funds of Hedge Funds and Market Indices 1990-2001

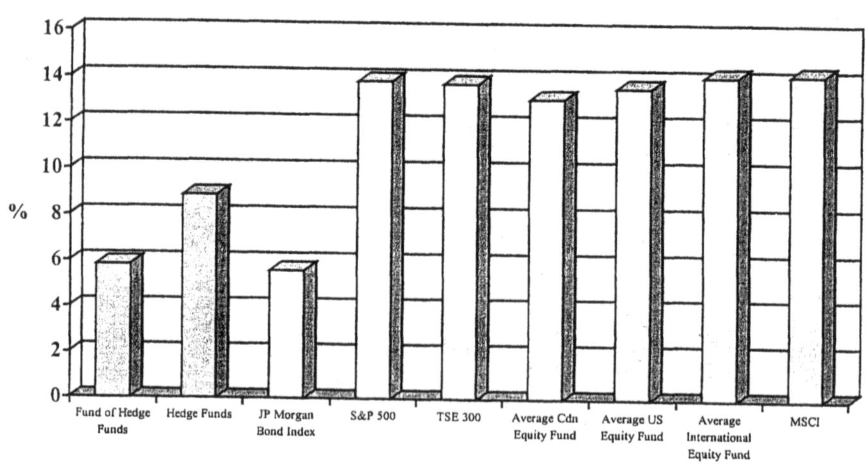

Source: MAR/LaPorte

By using an offshore fund, a U.S.-based hedge fund manager can reduce the burden of compliance with laws and regulations while employing dynamic and flexible trading strategies that mutual fund managers cannot. Mutual funds use buy-and-hold strategies, whereas hedge funds use strategies that are more dynamic in nature, such as short selling, derivatives, futures, options, concentrated investments, and currency trading. Schneeweis, Kazemi and Martin (2001) point out common misconceptions regarding the use of these strategies by hedge fund managers. Although one single hedge fund may not be diversified, investor risk across a number of hedge funds styles, or in a fund of hedge funds, is limited.

The fee structure of hedge funds is different from that of mutual funds. Hedge funds charge a management fee corresponding to 1 percent to 2 percent of assets under management. Most of their revenue, however, is generated from their performance fee, typically 20 percent of profits. Furthermore, these performance fees are often mitigated by high water marks and hurdle rates. On the other hand, mutual fund managers are typically paid on the amount of assets under management. Incentive fees are not offered to mutual fund managers, to discourage them from taking on undue risk. Thus, mutual fund managers are *passive* managers, whereas hedge fund managers are *active* managers.

HEDGE FUND DATABASES

Zurich Capital Markets, Hedge Fund Research (HFR) and TASS are the three leading hedge fund databases used by money mangers and academics. Data is collected on a monthly basis net of all management and performance fees, and will typically include additional information such as assets under management, leverage used, and redemption frequency. These databases are by no means complete. One study reported that more than 50 percent of hedge funds refrain from submitting monthly performance figures to database vendors (Chadha and Jansen (1998)). This must be kept in mind when evaluating strong claims regarding the hedge fund industry.

The ZCM and TASS databases contain the greatest number of dead hedge funds and are more suitable for academic studies, especially when survivorship bias is of interest. In constructing their hedge fund databases, vendors rely on hedge fund managers to voluntarily submit their returns, and are therefore subject to backfill, survivorship, selective, and non-reporting biases. Many database vendors have constructed their own hedge fund indices, but the methodology used in constructing and maintaining these indices will vary across databases.

HEDGE FUNDS BY STRATEGY

The goal of all hedge fund strategies, or "styles," is to maximize absolute returns in all types of market environments using differing levels of risk and return. Although the three major database providers (ZCM, HFR, and TASS) maintain their own classification of hedge fund strategies, they can usually be defined as being either *directional* or *non-directional* (Agarwal and Naik (2000b)). Hedge fund strategies having low correlation to stock markets are classified as non-directional (Market Neutral and Event Driven) while those having high correlation to stock markets are directional (global macro, long only, and short sellers).

To achieve their aim of absolute return, hedge funds use a wide range of strategies in various financial markets. This difference in style helps to distinguish various hedge funds. Data providers and researchers employ different classifications of hedge fund strategies. ZCM, for example, identifies ten hedge fund styles, while TASS and HFR each identify eleven.

A fund of hedge funds is a multi-manager hedge fund. While it allows for more diversification than a single fund, an extra layer of fees is incurred.

SIZE OF INDUSTRY

Because many hedge funds do not report their numbers to database vendors, it is difficult to determine the precise size of the industry. Moreover, there are overlaps of 30 to 35 percent across the major vendors. The President's Working Group on Financial Markets (1999) found 2,500 to 3,500 hedge funds in existence as of July 1998, managing capital of $250 billion. In January 2000, approximately 6,000 hedge funds held assets of around $600 billion, accounting for 4 percent of the $25 trillion held by institutions, pension funds, and endowment funds worldwide (Baily, Farrell and Lund (2000); deBrouwer (2001)). At the end of 2001, ZCM estimates of the hedge fund universe are 1,561 hedge funds holding $220 billion of assets under management, while estimates from HFR and TASS were 1,725 funds with $269 billion, and 1,895 funds with $260 billion, respectively. Professor Thomas Schneeweis of the University of Massachussets estimates that at the end of 2001, there were 4,000 hedge funds holding $550 billion in assets worldwide (Figure 1.5).

Figure 1.5
Hedge Fund Assets 1990-2001 ($USD Billion)

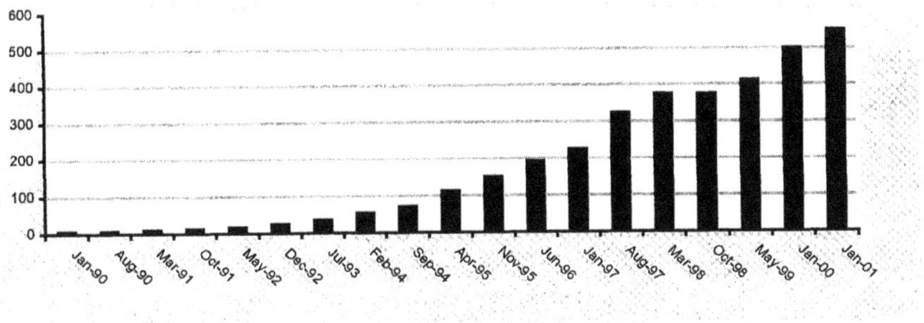

Source: Schneeweis (2001)

GROWTH IN HEDGE FUNDS

In 1968, there were 140 hedge funds in existence, and both their number and industry assets have experienced phenomenal growth since then, especially over the last ten years (Chadha and Jansen (1998)). Much of their capital is leveraged; by borrowing from banks' prime brokerage units, they were able to establish positions of approximately $4 trillion by 2000 (Stadlmann (2001)). Ian Morley, Director of Olympia Investments, attributes much of this growth to hedge funds' focus on positive returns and reduced risk during market declines (Morley (2001)). According to Van Hedge (1999), ZCM, TASS, and HFR, this growth rate apparently has tapered off since August 1998, partly as a result of the ensuing debacle in emerging markets. However, during 1999-2001, hedge funds generally outperformed market indices and mutual funds.

The President's Working Group and the Bank for International Settlements (BIS) have suggested guidelines for the largest 25 hedge funds with capital greater than $1 billion. There are a few hedge funds with assets greater than $5 billion. Moore Global Investments, a global macro fund managing $12 billion in capital at December 2001, was the world's largest at that time. It is estimated that by 2006, $1.7 trillion will be held by hedge funds worldwide (Rao and Szilagyi (1998)).

SECTION 1

HEDGE FUND PERFORMANCE

In this section of the book, we present studies that apply market timing and peer-analysis models to evaluate the performance of hedge funds and Commodities Trade Advisors (CTAs). In Chapter 2 we attempt to confirm the notion that hedge fund managers are deliberately avoiding market timing in their investment strategies. Using a sample of live and dead onshore and offshore funds, we find this to be the case in most of the hedge fund styles under consideration. We also find that most hedge fund styles exhibit good security selection ability, and that security selection tends to be negatively correlated with market timing ability, but not correlated with asset size or age of the fund. The results of our single-index and multi-index models are consistent with previous findings in the mutual fund literature. Previous studies have demonstrated that the return on hedge funds exhibits low correlation with those of market indices. Our results also demonstrate that most hedge funds do not exhibit market timing with these indices.

Chapter 3 examines the performance evaluation and market timing of the fund of hedge fund classification using conditioning of alphas and betas. We examine the selectivity and market timing skills of onshore and offshore funds of hedge funds (FOF) during the period 1993-2001. We use the Jensen selectivity index, the Treynor-Mazuy (TM) and Henriksson-Merton (HM) unconditional, and the respective conditional performance evaluation models. By conditioning alphas and betas, we investigate if FOF managers can select good hedge funds in times of changing economic conditions and if they can successfully interpret publicly available market information to their advantage. More specifically, we examine funds of hedge funds using active FOF benchmarks.

In Chapter 4 we use Data Envelopment Analysis (DEA) and apply the simple, cross-evaluation, and super-efficiency models to evaluate the performance of hedge fund classifications. The objective of alternative investment strategies such as hedge funds is to provide absolute returns, so using passive benchmarks to gauge their performance may be ineffective. DEA measures the efficiency of hedge funds so benchmarks do not have to be used. We evaluate the most efficient hedge funds in a risk/return framework. We examine only live hedge funds and determine which funds obtain superior efficiency scores.

In Chapter 5 we evaluate the performance of Commodities Trade Advisors (CTAs), another type of alternative investment currently gaining in popularity. Over the last ten years CTAs have performed poorly, but in recent extreme market events and negative S&P 500 months they have even outperformed hedge funds and market indices. Recently, pension funds have been increasing their exposure to CTAs as well as hedge funds as complementary alternative investments in traditional stock and bond portfolios.

Then, in Chapter 6 we examine the performance of the largest twenty funds of hedge funds from 1995-2002, to provide pension fund managers with simple descriptions of their risk/return characteristics. Various performance measures are presented to provide pension funds with a simple description of this popular alternative asset class currently gaining momentum in times of poorly performing markets. While the largest funds of funds do not necessarily perform better than smaller ones, their emphasis on due diligence and regular monitoring of their managers have allowed them to survive much longer.

CHAPTER 2

On the Market Timing of Hedge Fund Managers

INTRODUCTION

Research has shown that the majority of mutual fund managers are poor market timers. Is the same true for hedge fund managers? The assumption is that hedge fund managers do not seek to time the market. Our results show that most hedge fund styles do not reveal significant market-timing returns effects. We also investigate the correlation between market timing and security selection among hedge fund managers.

The attractiveness of hedge funds can be attributed in part to increased volatility in the stock and bond markets. Originally, hedge funds eschewed market-timing efforts (hence the term, hedge fund) and were focused instead on capturing relative pricing opportunities through arbitrage or other long/short trades. As time passed, however, a number of hedge fund managers began incorporating intentional market exposure and ultimately significant variations in that exposure.

With the impressive performance of hedge funds (mostly achieved during an unusually favorable equity market environment), it is now timely to ask whether hedge fund managers exhibit significant market timing activity. The answer should help investors formulate more rational expectations as to future returns and their sources.

THE CASE FOR HEDGE FUNDS

The benefits associated with the use of hedge funds to diversify traditional portfolios are well documented and seem well understood by investors (Fung and Hsieh (1999); Schneeweis and Spurgin (1998a); deBrouwer (2001)). Hedge funds provide a better risk-return trade-off, with less volatility and higher returns, than either bond or equity mutual funds

(Diz (2001)). The relatively low correlation of hedge funds to traditional stock, bond, and currency markets also provides added value in terms of downside equity risk management through diversification (Fung and Hsieh (1997); Schneeweis and Spurgin (1998b); Liang (1999); Agarwal and Naik (2000b); Gregoriou (2000); Ineichen (2002)). Most hedge fund styles do have some residual correlation (at times not insignificant) with equity markets (Brunel (2002)).

For taxable investors, hedge funds offer intriguing benefits in the construction of tax-efficient portfolios, particularly as their diversification enhances these benefits with less exposure to fixed-income instruments (Brunel (1999)). At the same time, however, they are notoriously tax-inefficient, as they generate most of their returns in the form of income and realized short-term capital gains, a challenge that tax efficient structures such as variable life insurance can help address (Lamm and Ghaleb-Harter (2001)).

The selection of a hedge fund manager is crucial to the investment process and should at a minimum incorporate detailed analysis of how the manager expects to create value (Anson (2000)). Many authors often assume *a priori* that hedge fund managers are avoiding market timing by maintaining hedged positions or focusing solely on security selection (alpha) while always remaining fully invested. But is this really the case?

THE EXPERIMENT

We used six benchmarks to evaluate the performance of hedge funds. Choosing an appropriate benchmark is critical, as pointed out by Roll (1978), Lehmann and Modest (1987), Grinblatt and Titman (1989), Rennie and Cowhey (1990), and Daniel, Grinblatt, Titman and Wermer (1997). We use the S&P 500, the Morgan Stanley World Capital International Index (MSCI), the Nasdaq 100, the Russell 2000, the Dow Jones Industrial Average (DJIA), and the U.S. Salomon Government Bond Index as market proxies. Including a bond index and a small-cap equity index substantially alters the sample alphas in their analysis of U.S. mutual funds, and a more recent study estimated the alpha against an extensive benchmark composed of passive and option-based strategies.

We chose the Nasdaq 100 rather than the Nasdaq Composite Index because roughly half the Russell 2000 Index stocks consist of Nasdaq-listed stocks. We also chose the DJIA over the S&P 500 index because the S&P and the Nasdaq Composite index are both dominated by large-cap stocks like Microsoft, Intel, and Cisco (in fact, 13 percent of S&P 500 stocks are listed on the Nasdaq Composite index).

Research on mutual funds suggests that funds investing in large-cap stocks show negative market timing abilities, while funds investing in small-cap stocks show positive market timing abilities (Kon (1983); Henriksson (1984), Chang and Lewellen (1985)). The Russell 2000 Index has been especially embraced by hedge fund managers as a benchmark for passive and active investment strategies, since secondary issues tend to exhibit signs of future growth (Frank Russell, Inc. (2001)). We used the MSCI in our models to capture the market timing and security selection capabilities of hedge funds with a global investment strategy. We also note the small-firm or size effect, according to which smaller firms tend to outperform larger ones on a historical basis (Banz (1981)).

LITERATURE REVIEW

The literature on the security selection and market timing of mutual fund managers is extensive (Kon and Chen (1979); Henriksson and Merton (1981); Merton (1981); Henriksson (1984)). Using a method developed from arbitrage pricing theory, Chang and Lewellen (1985) found that mutual fund portfolios do not outperform buy-and-hold strategies. Jagannathan and Korajczyk (1986) found that market timing skills are often negative and seldom positive. Yet Lehmann and Modest (1987), Cumby and Glen (1990), Lee and Rahman (1990), Grinblatt and Titman (1994), and Janjigian and Bello (1997) found evidence of good market timing and security selection.

According to Jagannathan and Korajczyk (1986) and Bollen and Busse (2001), the successful mutual fund manager increases allocations to equities before the market falls. Since hedge fund managers often use leverage to enhance portfolio returns, it stands to reason that their market timing ability would be positively correlated with systematic risk and that systematic risk would be amplified by the amount of leverage used. Most studies, however, suggest that a negative correlation between security selection and market timing is expected. This could be the result of misspecification of the market portfolio, or from neglecting to include certain factors in the model (Henriksson (1984)).

Do hedge fund managers have skill? Can they process information from global markets, and interpret changing economic conditions to add value or to improve their performance returns? The greater the performance persistence of returns, the more likely returns are due to manager skill than luck.

Another factor possibly related to manager skill is the underlying returns from the passive investment strategies followed (Schneeweis, Kazemi, and Martin (2001)). Brown, Goetzmann, and Ibbotson (1999) suggest that hedge fund managers show little evidence of differential manager skill and do not add value, but their study used annual returns and an inappropriate database with hand-collected data, so its results are less robust. However, Edwards and Caglayan (2001a) found that hedge fund managers possess good manager skills. Since hedge funds trade primarily in U.S. markets, they use the S&P 500, a U.S. small cap index and government bond indices in their multifactor model examining performance persistence.

Many authors have analyzed the performance persistence of hedge funds (Brorsen and Harri (1998); Schneeweis (1998); Ackermann, McEnally and Ravenscraft (1999); Brown, Goetzmann, and Ibbotson (1999); Agarwal and Naik (2000b); Asness, Krail, and Liew (2001)), but their results differ depending on the database and the time period used (Fung and Hsieh (2000); Liang (2000)). There is also evidence that mutual fund managers time their exposure to markets when the markets show low levels of volatility. This is consistent with the finding that hedge fund managers regularly modify the weights of the assets comprising their portfolios. Certain observers argue that a hedge fund manager's returns are usually comprised of three components: 1) the asset categories the manager invests in, 2) the hedge fund strategy, and 3) the use of leverage. Mutual fund managers, however, use only the first two.

A modified version of the Treynor-Mazuy model yields a greater proportion of negative market timing along with a negative correlation between market timing and security selection; however, the measurement of U.S. equity mutual fund performance varies depending on the benchmark used. Kon and Chen (1979) and Chang and Lewellen (1985) recognize these problems. Lehmann and Modest (1987), Grinblatt and Titman

(1989), and Elton, et al. (1993) find that the measurement of U.S. equity mutual fund performance varies depending on the benchmark used. Elton, et al. (1993) and Ferson and Schadt (1996) discuss some of the misspecification problems related to performance measurement that can arise when funds in a sample include assets from the benchmark index, such as international equities and bonds.

DATA AND METHODOLOGY

Our data consist of 1,494 live and 1,196 dead offshore and onshore hedge funds that reported monthly results (net of all fees) to the Zurich/LaPorte Asset Allocation System from January 1990 until December 2000. This database classifies hedge funds into ten different styles (definitions in Table 2.1).

Table 2.1
Definition of the Zurich/LaPorte Hedge Fund Styles

Global International	Manager pays attention to economic changes around the world (except in the U.S.)
Market Neutral	Half long/half short manager attempts to lock out or neutralize risk
Global Macro	Opportunistic trading manager who profits from changes in global economies, typically based on major interest rate shifts
Short Sellers	Manager takes a position that stock prices will go down. Used as a hedge for short-only portfolios
Long Only	Manager takes a position that stock prices will go up
Event Driven	Manager focuses on securities of companies in reorganization and bankruptcy, ranging from senior-secured debt to common stock
Fund of Funds	Capital is allocated among a number of hedge funds
Global Emerging	Manager invests in less mature financial markets. Because shorting is not permitted in many emerging markets, managers must go to cash or other markets when evaluations make being long unattractive
Global Established	Manager focuses on opportunities in established markets such as the U.S., Europe, and Japan
Sector	Follows specific economic sectors and/or industries. Managers can use a wide range of methodologies

Source: Ackermann, McEnally, and Ravenscraft (1999) and www.marhedge.com.

Table 2.2
Number of Live and Dead Hedge Funds in Zurich/LaPorte Database in Existence For At Least Thirty-Six Months, by Style of Hedge Fund

Hedge Fund Class	*Number of Live Funds*	*Number of Dead Funds*
Fund of Hedge Funds	240 (73%)	91 (27%)
Global Emerging	59 (76%)	19 (24%)
Global Established	216 (68%)	101 (32%)
Global International	37 (26%)	107 (74%)
Global Macro	39 (44%)	50 (56%)
Short Sellers	14 (58%)	10 (42%)
Event Driven	93 (70%)	39 (30%)
Long Only	12 (71%)	5 (29%)
Sector	56 (69%)	25 (31%)
Market Neutral	187 (67%)	94 (33%)

Source: *www.laportesoft.com*

Chi-square test : $\chi^2 = 129,\ df = 9,\ p = 0.0001$

We do not use funds with less than thirty-six months of returns. Defunct funds are included in our analyses to address the problem of survivorship bias. Summary statistics for the number of live and dead funds for each style are presented in Table 2.2. Only 541 of the 1,196 dead hedge funds reported returns for at least thirty-six months, which implies that many funds stop reporting returns in the short term because of poor performance, or because they do not want to attract additional capital. The chi-square test confirms that there are significant differences in the proportion of dead funds within each class ($p = 0.0001$), ranging from 24 percent of the Global Emerging funds to 74 percent of the Global International funds (Table 2.2).

Treynor and Mazuy (1966) argue that if a manager could predict market returns successfully, he would purchase a greater amount of the market portfolio when the return on the market is high and a smaller proportion when it is low. Since the betas of hedge fund managers constantly change and their portfolio weights are not usually known, the Treynor-Mazuy model (hereinafter referred to as the TM model) may prove ideal for market timing. However, identifying an appropriate benchmark model is always difficult because hedge fund managers trade frequently and use dynamic strategies, including derivative instruments and investing in different asset classes. It is further complicated by the fact that hedge funds tend to display non-linear exposures to standard asset markets (Agarwal and Naik (2000a)).

The TM model requires that hedge fund returns not be co-skewed with the benchmark return. This is because passive investors who choose assets that are co-skewed with the benchmark will erroneously be recorded as successful market timers, without actually possessing any market timing abilities (Zechner (2000)). The TM model not only examines the likelihood of these inherent biases, but also analyzes the sources of hedge fund performance (Brunel (2002)).

Table 2.3A
Regressions for TM Model (1), by Hedge Fund Style
For S&P 500 Index, 1990-2000

Estimate (t-statistic)	α_p	β_1	β_2	*Adjusted* R^2
Event Driven	1.0511	0.2688	-0.0265	
	(16.98)***	(22.31)***	(-15.22)***	0.07
Fund of Funds	0.6214	0.2421	-0.0165	
	(23.31)***	(46.56)***	(-22.00)***	0.11
Global Emerging	0.8633	0.7067	-0.0522	
	(5.45)***	(24.24)***	(-12.70)***	0.15
Global Established	0.8969	0.6168	-0.0179	
	(17.49)***	(61.59)***	(-12.56)***	0.15
Global International	0.8905	0.4757	-0.0339	
	(4.95)***	(11.74)***	(-5.44)***	0.02
Global Macro	0.6336	0.3124	-0.0096	
	(7.20)***	(17.02)***	(-3.58)***	0.05
Long Only	0.6348	0.9077	-0.0218	
	(1.88)	(14.52)***	(-2.44)**	0.18
Market Neutral	0.8698	0.0850	-0.0095	
	(21.29)***	(10.81)***	(-8.46)***	0.01
Sector	1.7975	0.7128	-0.0299	
	(12.06)***	(26.19)***	(-7.80)***	0.14
Short Sellers	0.5857	-0.9506	0.0281	
	(2.53)**	(-20.57)***	(4.23)***	0.20

*** Significant at the 0.001 level. ** Significant at the 0.01 level.
* Significant at the 0.05 level.

Our modified version of the TM model adjusts for additional market indices and measures both market timing skill (β_2 for the DJIA, β_4 for the U.S. Bond Index) and security selection ability (α_p) of hedge fund managers. Both TM models used in this paper are described in the Appendix at the end of this chapter.

Table 2.3B
Regressions for TM Model (1), by Hedge Fund Style for Morgan Stanley World Capital International Index, 1990-2000

Estimate (t-statistic)	α_p	β_1	β_2	*Adjusted* R^2
Event	1.0267	0.2808	-0.0230	
Driven	(16.73)***	(21.61)***	(-11.49)***	0.07
Fund of	0.5948	0.2758	-0.0129	
Funds	(22.71)***	(49.17)***	(-15.04)***	0.11
Global	0.6877	0.8463	-0.0425	
Emerging	(4.47)***	(26.35)***	(-8.87)***	0.16
Global	0.9973	0.6484	-0.0134	
Established	(19.61)***	(59.94)***	(-8.15)***	0.15
Global	0.9730	0.4576	-0.0272	
International	(5.41)***	(11.09)***	(-3.99)***	0.02
Global	0.7604	0.2869	-0.0096	
Macro	(8.63)***	(14.94)***	(-3.19)**	0.04
Long	0.8334	0.9885	-0.0196	
Only	(2.52)*	(14.31)***	(-1.88)	0.18
Market	0.8536	0.1002	-0.0088	
Neutral	(21.26)***	(11.71)***	(-6.77)***	0.01
Sector	1.7720	0.8128	-0.0224	
	(12.2)***	(26.97)***	(-4.99)***	0.15
Short	0.3130	-0.9465	0.0252	
Sellers	(1.35)	(-19.54)***	(3.38)***	0.20

*** *Significant at the 0.001 level.* ** *Significant at the 0.01 level.* * *Significant at the 0.05 level.*

Finally, we use the Pearson product moment correlation coefficient (r) to investigate the linear relationship between security selection and market timing, and the variables hedge fund size (amount of assets) and age (defined from inception date).

EMPIRICAL RESULTS

We fit three TM models (1) to each class of hedge fund as defined in Table 2.1, using the S&P 500, MSCI, and DJIA indices individually as market proxies. The results are shown in Tables 2.3A through 2.3C.

Table 2.3C
Regressions for TM Model (1), by Hedge Fund Style for Dow Jones Industrial Average Index, 1 990-2000

Estimate (t-statistic)	α_p	β_1	β_2	*Adjusted* R^2
Event	0.8830	0.2464	-0.0154	
Driven	(14.20)***	(20.83)***	(-9.47)***	0.05
Fund of	0.5623	0.2056	-0.0103	
Funds	(20.91)***	(40.20***	(-14.80)***	0.08
Global	0.6005	0.7039	-0.0354	
Emerging	(3.84)***	(24.84)***	(-9.46)***	0.14
Global	0.8755	0.5004	-0.0991	
Established	(16.73)***	(50.14)***	(-6.77)***	0.10
Global	0.8675	0.4424	-0.0299	
International	(4.75)***	(11.32)***	(-5.06)***	0.02
Global	0.5823	0.2768	-0.0044	
Macro	(6.56)***	(15.53)***	(-1.75)	0.04
Long	0.6740	0.6790	-0.0083	
Only	(1.94)	(10.77)***	(-0.98)	0.10
Market	0.8060	0.0709	-0.0049	
Neutral	(19.91)***	(9.33)***	(-4.77)***	0.01
Sector	1.7781	0.5047	-0.0145	
	(11.70)***	(18.52)***	(-4.03)***	0.07
Short	0.6973	-0.7658	0.0114	
Sellers	(2.89)**	(-16.29)***	(1.76)	0.13

*** *Significant at the 0.001 level.* ** *Significant at the 0.01 level.* * *Significant at the 0.05 level.*

The coefficients of the TM model differ according to which class is considered, rather than by which index is used as the market proxy. We find that all estimated values of security selection are positive ($\alpha_p > 0$) , but vary according to style. The sector funds demonstrate the best security selection ($\alpha_p \approx 1.8$), while the Short Sellers demonstrate the worst when the S&P 500 and MSCI are used.

Event Driven is the only other class with security selection coefficient greater than one $(\alpha_p > 0)$; however, the low R-squared value observed implies that this is true only in a fraction of the funds. We find evidence of good market timing within the Short Sellers style only, as this style has a positive and significant market timing coefficient ($\beta_2 \approx 0.03$ for S&P 500 and MSCI, $\beta_2 \approx 0.01$ for DJIA). It is the only style with negative effects of systematic risk $\alpha_p > 0$ coupled with positive market timing effect $(\beta_1 > 0)$, implying that returns r_{pt} are highest when the market returns r_{mt} are negative. This result is not surprising, since the Short Sellers are designed to profit from market downturns.

Most of the coefficients in Tables 3A through 3C are significant, but the low values of the adjusted R-squared, ranging from 0.02 to 0.20, indicate that the predictive power of these models is generally poor and confirm the notion that most hedge fund managers are avoiding market timing effects. The adjusted R-squared values are highest in the Short Sellers and Long Only styles, which can be explained by the directional strategies inherent in these funds.

The results of the modified TM Model are presented in Table 2.4 for each hedge fund style, and include an estimate of the regression coefficient, its corresponding *t*-statistic, and its corresponding VIF.

The results indicate that all hedge fund classes, except Global Emerging and Long Only, show good security selection skill $(\alpha_p > 0)$, with the Short Sellers ranking among the best.

We find evidence of inferior market timing in the Event Driven, Fund of Funds, Global International, Global Macro, and Market Neutral styles (either $\beta_2 < 0$ or $\beta_4 < 0$, or both). The Global Emerging style shows superior market timing with the Bond Index $(\beta_4 = 0.1509)$, but inferior market timing with the DJIA $(\beta_4 = -0.0178)$. Most of the styles have positive coefficients for systematic risk $(\beta_5, \beta_6, \beta_7)$, indicating that the returns on these funds tend to follow our selected benchmarks. Indeed, only the Event Driven style has a negative beta $(\beta_5 = -0.0271)$, and only the Short Sellers style has negative values of systematic risk, indicating that the funds in this style have benefited from negative returns on all three benchmarks.

The Russell 2000 is the only index with a positive regression coeffi-

Table 2.4
Regressions for Modified TM Model (2), by Hedge Fund Style for Various Market Indices, 1990-2000

Estimate (t-statistic) (VIF)	α_p *Intercept*	β_1 *DJIA*	β_2 *DJIA²*	β_3 *BOND*	β_4 *BOND²*	β_5 *Nasdaq 100*	β_6 *MSCI*	β_7 *Russell 2000*	C_p	*Adjusted* R^2
Event Driven	0.8791	0.0679	–0.0095	–0.0309	–0.0538	–0.0271	0.0187	0.2842		
	(13.02)***	(3.35)***	(–5.74)***	(–0.68)	(–2.13)*	(–2.91)**	(0.73)	(20.42)***		
		(3.14)	(1.11)	(1.15)	(1.14)	(2.52)	(4.21)	(2.40)	30.6	0.11
Fund of Funds	0.5512	–0.0089	–0.0052	–0.0246	–0.0693	0.0266	0.0856	0.1818		
	(19.29)***	(–1.02)	(–7.56)***	(–1.28)	(–6.56)***	(6.80)***	(7.62)***	(30.94)***		
		(3.24)	(1.11)	(1.15)	(1.15)	(2.51)	(4.47)	(2.38)	48.3	0.17
Global Emerging	0.2885	0.2851	–0.0178	–1.2070	0.1509	0.0064	0.2512	0.4024		
	(1.72)	(5.55)***	(–4.72)***	(–10.57)***	(2.34)**	(0.29)	(3.51)***	(12.41)***		
		(3.66)	(1.13)	(1.13)	(1.16)	(2.63)	(5.61)	(2.37)	8.9	0.21
Global Established	0.5998	0.0084	0.0015	–0.1955	0.0012	0.1221	0.1558	0.3767		
	(11.06)***	(0.51)	(1.12)	(–5.39)***	(0.06)	(16.36)***	(7.46)***	(33.69)***		
		(3.20)	(1.12)	(1.14)	(1.14)	(2.50)	(4.34)	(2.41)	10.3	0.24
Global International	0.7931	0.1416	–0.0217	–0.0817	0.0128	–0.0282	0.1341	0.3181		
	(3.88)***	(2.09)*	(–3.54)***	(–0.61)	(0.18)	(–0.82)	(1.88)	(6.35)***		
		(3.02)	(1.09)	(1.22)	(1.13)	(2.47)	(3.04)	(2.53)	6.8	0.02
Global Macro	0.6379	0.0986	–0.0016	0.3539	–0.1339	0.0276	–0.0319	0.2102		
	(6.51)***	(3.27)**	(–0.62)	(5.45)***	(–3.78)***	(1.87)	(–0.91)	(9.60)***		
		(2.98)	(1.10)	(1.17)	(1.14)	(2.48)	(3.55)	(2.48)	10.1	0.07
Long Only	0.0588	–0.0767	0.0034	0.0172	0.0576	0.2302	0.2522	0.5319		
	(0.17)	(–0.74)	(0.43)	(0.07)	(0.43)	(5.10)***	(1.75)	(7.94)***		
		(3.52)	(1.13)	(1.14)	(1.16)	(2.60)	(5.31)	(2.36)	12.5	0.29
Market Neutral	0.8003	–0.0238	–0.0023	0.0104	–0.0329	0.0017	0.0163	0.1190		
	(17.75)***	(–1.74)	(–2.14)*	(0.34)	(–1.94)	(0.27)	(0.90)	(13.02)***		
		(3.35)	(1.12)	(1.14)	(1.15)	(2.49)	(4.70)	(2.38)	24.7	0.02
Sector	1.2407	–0.1854	0.0003	–0.1256	–0.0235	0.2128	0.1579	0.5625		
	(8.32)***	(–4.05)***	(0.10)	(–1.24)	(–0.41)	(10.94)***	(2.45)**	(19.64)***		
		(3.76)	(1.14)	(1.13)	(1.15)	(2.64)	(5.82)	(2.36)	13.8	0.29
Short Sellers	1.2580	0.1326	–0.0053	0.4768	–0.0730	–0.3032	–0.2322	–0.5863		
	(5.44)***	(1.92)	(0.91)	(3.11)**	(–0.86)	(–9.09)***	(–2.89)**	(–11.81)***		
		(2.99)	(1.11)	(1.15)	(1.14)	(2.54)	(3.61)	(2.49)	15.5	0.37

*** Significant at the 0.001 level. ** Significant at the 0.01 level. * Significant at the 0.05 level.

cient ($\beta_1 > 0$) for all styles except Short Sellers. This suggests that hedge fund returns are most consistently influenced by the Russell 2000 index. Judging by the magnitude of the estimated coefficient, this is especially true for hedge funds in the Short Sellers ($\beta_1 = -0.5863$), Sector ($\beta_1 = -0.5625$), and Long Only ($\beta_1 = -0.5319$) styles.

The fit of this model is substantially superior to the TM model (1), as evidenced by the values of the adjusted R-squared, which range from 0.02 for Market Neutral to 0.37 for Short Sellers. Unacceptably high values of Mallow's C_p are found in those styles with low values of the adjusted R-squared, especially in the Fund of Funds, Event Driven, and Market Neutral styles. We find little evidence of collinearity among the independent variables. Indeed, most of the VIFs are reasonably small. The condition numbers are all under 4 (these data are not presented).

As expected, we find evidence of negative correlation between selected parameters of the modified TM model (2). The results in Table 2.5 point to strong negative correlation between security selection and market timing with the U.S. Bond Index, especially within the Long Only ($r = -0.8643$) and Short Sellers ($r = -0.6895$) styles, and between security selection and market timing with the DJIA, especially within the Short Sellers ($r = -0.7346$) and Global Emerging ($r = -0.6688$) styles. Consistent with most studies on mutual funds, this provides further evidence that managers are good at security selection and poor at market timing. We find evidence of the same pattern in hedge fund managers, but the results are tempered by the low R-squared values of the models from which the parameters are obtained.

Table 2.6 presents correlations between security selection and market timing effects with the DJIA and the U.S. Bond Index estimated from model (2), and variables corresponding to average asset size and age (calculated from inception date).

Most of these correlations are not significant at the 0.05 level. However, we find evidence of correlation between asset size and U.S. Bond Index market timing effect within the Short Sellers ($r = 0.6488$) and Global Macro ($r = -0.2382$) styles, and also between asset size and security selection within these two styles ($r = -0.4407$ for Short Sellers and $r = -0.2486$ for Global Macro).

Table 2.5
Average Performance Measures and Correlations for Modified TM Model (2), By Hedge Fund Style

	Parameters from Modified TM Model (2)			*Pearson Correlation Coefficient (r)*	
Hedge Fund Style	*Security Selection (α_p)*	*Market Timing DJIA (β_2)*	*Market Timing US Bond Index (β_4)*	*α_p and β_2*	*α_p and β_4*
Event Driven	0.8551 (0.0001)	-0.0083 (0.0001)	-0.0582 (0.0366)	-0.3522 (0.0001)	-0.5151 (0.0001)
Fund of Funds	0.5547 (0.0001)	-0.0061 (0.0001)	-0.0552 (0.0001)	-0.1610 (0.0034)	-0.4094 (0.0001)
Global Emerging	0.3951 (0.0546)	-0.0174 (0.0048)	0.0836 (0.1715)	-0.6688 (0.0001)	-0.3344 (0.0028)
Global Established	0.6403 (0.0001)	0.0034 (0.0848)	0.0003 (0.9884)	-0.2371 (0.0001)	-0.3538 (0.0001)
Global International	0.6991 (0.0001)	-0.0300 (0.0001)	0.0415 (0.3803)	-0.2623 (0.0015)	-0.2245 (0.0068)
Global Macro	0.5374 (0.0001)	-0.0010 (0.8565)	-0.0856 (0.0047)	-0.5916 (0.0001)	-0.2679 (0.0111)
Long Only	-0.0864 (0.7701)	0.0059 (0.3290)	0.1022 (0.4205)	0.0387 (0.8829)	-0.8643 (0.0001)
Market Neutral	0.7980 (0.0001)	-0.0022 (0.2042)	-0.0315 (0.0504)	-0.3594 (0.0001)	-0.1445 (0.0153)
Sector	1.3925 (0.0001)	-0.0004 (0.8973)	-0.0769 (0.1830)	-0.4069 (0.0002)	-0.5530 (0.0001)
Short Sellers	1.7098 (0.0001)	-0.0154 (0.1496)	-0.1070 (0.1085)	-0.7346 (0.0001)	-0.6895 (0.0003)

Numbers are parameter estimates from modified TM model (2), and coefficients of correlation between α_p and β_2 as well as between α_p and β_4, along with corresponding p-values.

SUMMARY AND CONCLUSION

Using the single-index TM model (1), we find that, as expected, most hedge fund styles are not good market timers. However, we find evidence of superior market timing within the Short Sellers style. This is also the only style with a negative estimate of systematic risk ($\beta_1 < 0$). We find that there is good security selection in all styles.

However, as noted earlier, hedge funds use dynamic trading strategies and strongly shift their factor exposures, so evaluating their performance relative to any market proxy is difficult. This could partially explain the low R-squared values seen when our model is fitted to the data.

Our three main findings are as follows:

- First, all hedge fund styles rely on good security selection skills, with the sector and event driven classifications at the top of the list. Since these styles are specialized in the selection of securities, the latter style is more focused on security selection, as events are, by definition, security rather than market specific.
- Second, hedge funds seem to derive little or no benefit from varying their net market exposure levels – an interesting finding since so many managers do vary their market exposures – but this may reflect an unintentional, bottom-up, market exposure variation rather a top down process.
- Finally, the funds seem more directly related to the small-cap universe, an interesting finding, as it would confirm the concentration of many strategies in that area, but a surprising one in the event-driven, arbitrage, and short-seller styles, where one would actually assume more of a large to midcap bias.

Our research differs from other mutual fund studies because we use a modified quadratic regression of the Treynor-Mazuy model to capture non-linearities in beta resulting from market timing activities. Since hedge fund strategies are dynamic in nature, the TM model produces a better fit and measures market timing skills as well as security selection abilities.

Our analysis investigates the effects of the size of hedge fund holdings. To verify the robustness of our results, we repeated the market timing tests using the Henriksson and Merton model. The results were similar (we do not present them here).

One drawback to our study is that hedge fund database vendors only provide monthly data, so we were unable to obtain daily data, which provide better estimates and help increase the power of tests (Kothari and Warner (2001)), but only a handful of hedge funds trading on various exchanges provide daily NAVs. Zurich/LaPorte provides data on a monthly basis, net of management and performance fees. Other database vendors also supply monthly data, but the classification of hedge fund styles may differ across databases.

Goetzmann, Ingersoll, and Ivkovic (2000), and Bollen and Busse (2001) explain that monthly data may fail to properly capture the market timing activities of the manager, since managers trade more frequently than simply on a monthly basis. In performance persistence studies, survivorship and other biases such as instant history bias, selection bias, and backfill bias are found to be different across hedge fund databases, a problem that can lead to mixed results.

To the authors' knowledge, we are the first to investigate the security selection abilities and market timing skills of hedge fund managers. Our results indicate that most hedge fund styles show good security selection abilities, but no significant market timings effects. We present some possible explanations:

1. Hedge funds that invest in large-cap stocks normally display inferior market timing skills, while hedge funds investing in small-cap stocks (such as in the Russell 2000 index) display superior market timing skills and negative security selection abilities. Hedge fund managers tend to look for higher returns in small-cap stocks because they are inefficiently priced; large-cap stocks are priced better, making it more difficult to time entry and exit.
2. Skillful active managers are more likely to outperform the small-cap indices than their large-cap colleagues. Approximately 75 percent of active small-cap managers outperformed their benchmarks over the past three years; 22 percent of active large-cap managers outperformed the S&P 500 during that time (Frank Russell, Inc. (2001)).
3. Over the course of the 1991-1998 bull market, the indices used here recorded eight years of positive returns in an expanding global economy. Therefore, over our examination period, it has not been arduous for some small hedge funds to time the market well.

The interaction of market timing and security selection skill is complex, and there is considerable need for future research, particularly with regard to causes and consequences. We particularly need to evaluate the difference between international and residual net market exposure variation; the former reflects an active decision and the latter is simply a consequence of security selection activity.

Our conclusions are similar to those previously found for mutual fund managers, and we found no difference when using the TM model or the modified TM model. The results demonstrate that only certain styles of hedge funds exhibit significant market timing effects in a multi-index model (especially the short-sellers), confirming that the returns of most hedge funds have low correlation with stock and bond market indices.

Table 2.6
Pearson Correlation Coefficient (r)
Between Parameters from TM Model (2) and Variables
Corresponding to Asset Size and Age, By Style of Hedge Fund

Correlation Coefficient (p-value)	*Security Selection (α_p)*	*Market Timing with DJIA (β_2)*	*Market Timing with US Bond Index (β_4)*
	Event Driven		
Average Asset Size	0.0190	0.0671	-0.0360
	(0.8299)	(0.4462)	(0.6836)
Age	0.0348	-0.0593	-0.0306
	(0.6931)	(0.5011)	(0.7287)
Fund of Funds			
Average Asset Size	0.0822	-0.0525	-0.1042
	(0.1363)	(0.3419)	(0.0587)
Age	-0.0430	0.0261	-0.0624
	(0.4368)	(0.6372)	(0.2581)
	Global Emerging		
Average Asset Size	0.1412	-0.0482	0.0076
	(0.2175)	(0.6751)	(0.9472)
Age	-0.0802	-0.0289	0.1870
	(0.4854)	(0.8018)	(0.1011)
Global Established			
Average Asset Size	0.0423	-0.0866	-0.0207
	(0.4529)	(0.1238)	(0.7138)
Age	-0.0219	-0.1988	0.0021
	(0.6982)	(0.0004)	(0.9701)
	Global International		
Average Asset Size	0.0942	0.0170	-0.1166
	(0.2613)	(0.8398)	(0.1639)
Age	0.1222	0.0977	-0.0710
	(0.1445)	(0.2443)	(0.3979)
Global Macro			
Average Asset Size	0.2486	-0.0529	-0.2382
	(0.0188)	(0.6225)	(0.0246)
Age	0.2067	-0.0412	-0.2333
	(0.0520)	(0.7015)	(0.0278)
	Long Only		
Average Asset Size	0.2362	-0.1804	-0.1701
	(0.3613)	(0.4883)	(0.5141)
Age	0.4223	-0.4093	-0.1980
	(0.0913)	(0.1028)	(0.4462)

		Market Neutral	
Average Asset Size	0.0215	-0.0952	-0.0234
	(0.7196)	(0.1115)	(0.6963)
Age	0.0124	-0.0994	0.0328
	(0.8363)	(0.0963)	(0.5839)
		Sector	
Average Asset Size	0.0192	0.0414	0.1258
	(0.8648)	(0.7139)	(0.2630)
Age	-0.1198	-0.0212	0.1216
	(0.2868)	(0.8510)	(0.2797)
		Short Sellers	
Average Asset Size	-0.4407	0.0835	0.6488
	(0.0353)	(0.7048)	(0.0008)
Age	-0.5718	0.3943	0.2286
	(0.0044)	(0.0626)	(0.2941)

We hope that future authors will address how to more efficiently examine all the facets of hedge fund manager performance and make it easier to compare mutual fund and hedge fund manager performance.

Appendix

The Treynor-Mazuy (TM) model is defined as:

$$r_{pt} = \alpha_p + \beta_1 r_{mt} + \beta_2 r_{mt}^2 + \varepsilon_{pt} \tag{1}$$

where

t = time period,

r_{pt} = excess rate of return (observed minus risk-free) on hedge fund p during period t,

α_p = estimate of selectivity performance of hedge fund manager,

β_1 = estimate of systematic risk,

r_{mt} = excess rate of return on the market index during period t,

β_2 = estimate of market timing performance, and

ε_{pt} = random error term for hedge fund p in period t (unsystematic risk in portfolio).

The method that the TM model uses to evaluate portfolio performance has been discussed extensively. Under certain conditions, the TM model adequately measures the market timing ability of fund managers and it has been argued that that a positive value of β_2 represents superior market timing ability because it indicates that the returns of the portfolio are more responsive to positive than negative market returns. If no market timing is found, then $\beta_2 = 0$, while a negative value of β_2 represents inferior market timing.

Indeed, since $r_{mt}^2 > 0$, a positive value of β_2 in Equation (1) ensures that r_{pt} will not substantially decrease when $r_{mt} < 0$. Conversely, when $\beta_2 < 0$, r_{pt} will decrease faster than when $\beta_2 \geq 0$. Therefore, in the TM model, the negative effect of market downturns on portfolio returns is mitigated in those managers with superior market timing ability, but amplified in those with inferior market timing ability.

A model that isolates the effects of non-Dow assets held by hedge funds would be useful to better explain the variability of hedge fund returns. This can be achieved by adding a bond index along with other equity indices in the regression. Thus, the TM model is altered to assess the market timing of hedge funds with the DJIA and U.S. bond index simultaneously, while adjusting for the Nasdaq 100, MSCI, and Russell 2000. We propose the following characterization for the hedge fund returns:

$$r_{pt} = \alpha_p + \beta_1 r_{dt} + \beta_2 r_{dt}^2 + \beta_3 r_{bt} + \beta_4 r_{bt}^2 + \beta_5 rn + \beta_6 r_{mt} + \beta_7 r_{rt} + \varepsilon_{pt} \quad (2)$$

where

t = time period,

r_{pt} = excess rate of return on hedge fund p during period t,

α_p = estimate of selectivity performance by the hedge fund manager,

$\beta_1, \beta_3, \beta_5, \beta_6, \beta_7$ = estimates of systematic risk,

r_{dt} = excess rate of return on the DJIA during period t,

β_2, β_4 = estimates of market timing effect for DJIA and U.S. Bond Index respectively,

r_{bt} = excess rate of return on the Salomon U.S. Government Bond Index (all maturities) during period t,

r_{nt} = excess rate of return on the Nasdaq 100 Index during period t,

r_{mt} = excess rate of return on the MSCI during period t,

r_{rt} = excess rate of return on the Russell 2000 Index during period t, and

ε_{pt} = random error term for hedge fund p in period t.

We use several measures of goodness-of-fit in our analyses. Mallow's C_p, like the adjusted R-squared, measures how well a model fits given data. A value of C_p close to p, where p is the number of variables in the model, indicates that the model does not suffer from substantial bias. Variance inflation factors (VIF) and condition numbers (CN) are used to detect collinearity among the independent variables on the right-hand side of Equation (2). Condition numbers greater than 30 indicate collinearity is present; values of VIF > 4 indicate that collinearity could be present; and values of VIF > 10 indicate that collinearity is both present and likely to pose a serious problem.

CHAPTER 3

Performance Evaluation of Funds of Hedge Funds Using Conditional Alphas and Betas

INTRODUCTION

Over the past decade of increasing market volatility, fund of hedge funds (FOFs) – diversified portfolio of hedge funds – have become an attractive alternative asset classes for pension funds, university endowments, and high net worth individuals (LHabitant (2002)). FOFs can reduce downside risk through diversification of negatively, low and non-correlated hedge fund managers. Japan's Sumitomo Life insurance company is currently investing $3 billion into twenty-eight FOFs (Clow (2002)). FOFs increased their market share by 50 per- cent between 1996 and 2002 being preferred over hedge funds because investors are more inclined to have an external consulting team for selecting hedge funds and, in exchange, give a portion of profits and returns to the consulting team. In terms of popularity, the numbers indicate that there have been more FOFs created than hedge funds (Clow (2002)).

Many things account for the increase in popularity of hedge funds and FOFs, including the lacklustre stock market performance since 1998 and the Nasdaq sell off. FOFs provide access to a wider variety of hedge fund managers and eliminate the burden of selecting managers. The fact that the majority of pension funds and university endowments do not possess the knowledge or resources to set up proprietary portfolios of hedge funds has also fuelled the industry (Acito and Fisher (2002)).

During 1993-2001, FOFs outperformed the S&P 500 Index on a risk-adjusted basis. Because FOFs deliver more consistent returns with lower volatility than individual hedge funds, they are ideal for diversifying traditional portfolios (da Costa (2001)). Over this past decade, pension funds have been allocating an increasing amount of their assets to FOFs to diversify their portfolios and are quickly becoming permanent fixtures in pension fund portfolios for downside equity risk management (deBrouwer (2001)) and Schneeweis, Spurgin and Potter (1996)).

Research shows it is risky to hold a few hedge funds in a portfolio, but a portfolio of 15 to 25 hedge funds can reduce the risk to bond levels and maintain constant returns between 7 and 15 percent per year (Fothergill and Coke (2001), Lamm (1999) and Peskin, et al. (2000)). By using hedge fund managers with varying investment strategies, FOFs are able to provide investors with a 'hedge' against market drops and an important reduction in downside risk. However, each FOFs manager has his own recipe for manager selection; therefore, an inadequately chosen portfolio of hedge funds with sub-optimal results is not infrequent. One must not forget the demise of Long-Term Capital Management (LTCM) in August of 1998 and the closing of Tiger Management in March of 2000, which reminded investors of the benefits of diversifying among different hedge funds and especially FOFs.

As of December 31, 2001, FOFs represented 23 percent (in terms of assets) of the hedge fund universe, according to Zurich Capital Markets database (ZCM). While the number of hedge funds hovers around 6,000 with an estimated $600 billion in capital, FOFs number around 600 with about $100-$120 billion in capital, according to Acito and Fisher (2002). The authors also estimate that 70 percent of FOF investors are American, 15 percent European, 10 percent Japanese, and 5 percent other.

The main drawback of FOFs is the extra layer of management and performance fees the specialist charges as compensation for his knowledge and skills in selecting, rebalancing and monitoring hedge fund managers (Anson (2000)). Another drawback is that a FOF with an excessive number of hedge funds (>40), on average, will produce low standard deviation, low skewness, dilute manage skill (alpha), and will closely resemble a FOF index (Amin and Kat (2002b)). The risk management techniques, styles, and analysis of individual hedge fund managers are constantly monitored by a FOF manager on a daily, weekly and monthly basis (Acito and Fisher (2002)). Leveraged Capital Holdings (LCH) was the first Fund of Hedge Funds created in 1969 by Rothschild Asset Management of Zurich. It has outperformed the S&P 500 Index since its inception and its manager, George Karlweis, retired after 30 years as its managing director. LCH with almost US $1.2 billion in assets trades daily on the Amsterdam Stock Exchange and one share can be purchased at $153 US (at the time of this writing). ALTIN with $400 million in assets is also a well-known and established FOF that trades daily on the Swiss Stock Exchange. Both LCH and ALTIN have approximately 25-30 top hedge fund managers and are actively managed.

The cost of investing in a well-known and established FOF can be higher than the cost of building, monitoring, and maintaining a proprietary portfolio of hedge funds. But, properly chosen FOFs are attractive diversifiers because they allow investors to benefit from numerous managers who spread investment risk across a wide range of hedge fund strategies (Schneeweis and Spurgin (2000)). Individually, the hedge fund strategies can experience significant return variability, but when combined, they tend to be more stable (Fung and Hsieh (1999, 2002)).

FOFs have grown in popularity over this last decade because of their specialized investment strategies and objectives (Gregoriou and Rouah (2002)). FOF managers can trade a portfolio of hedge funds when they believe a change in the direction of the market is occurring. The logic is that a well-diversified FOF manager can take advantage of market-specific risks while maintaining low correlations to stock, bond and currency markets. If the FOF manager's forecast is correct, he will provide superior returns and generate alpha (manager skill) (Ineichen (2002)). In addition, an important advantage of using the FOF classification is that it suffers the least from any biases and is less sensitive to measurement bias than traditional hedge fund indices produced by database vendors (Fung and Hsieh (2002)).

FOFs invest in other hedge funds with different styles and constantly monitor managers, which relieves pension funds and university endowments of the complicated selection and allocation process. In addition, FOFs do not compare themselves to traditional benchmarks. Rather, they are absolute performers like hedge funds. However, a great majority of FOFs are geographically diversified and use the Morgan Stanley Capital International World Index (MSCI) as a benchmark to provide some type of comparison for investors.

FOF managers have been known to time the markets by altering portfolio reallocations, rebalancing the weights of hedge fund managers as a result of incoming cash flow, and by actively managing portfolios on an ongoing basis. (Sharpe (1999) and Ineichen (2001)). As the number of FOF managers increases, the gap between inferior and superior performance is also increasing.

This Chapter examines whether FOF managers are good market timers in a predictive sense and thereby add value (select good hedge funds). Ineichen (2002) believes the value added is due to manager selection and monitoring of hedge fund managers rather than simply portfolio construction. Anson (2000) believes that only portfolio construction plays an important role in creating a successful FOF.

When examining the historical performance of FOFs, the data reveal that they are not affected by many of the idiosyncratic biases quoted from database vendors (Fung and Hsieh (2002)). Backfill bias does not exist in our study since we commence the analysis in 1993. Prior to this period, the Zurich Capital markets database previously called MAR started operations in 1993 and backfilled some hedge fund returns

When some hedge funds decide to stop reporting their numbers to database vendors – either because of the capital limit they have reached or poor performance – the likely result is survivorship bias for a traditional hedge fund index. On the other hand, a FOF manager holding a hedge fund in his portfolio will remain in the historical performance of the FOF, even if the hedge fund stops reporting to database vendors; hence, there is no selection bias and lower survivorship bias than hedge funds (Fung and Hsieh (2002)). Whenever a FOF manager adds or removes a hedge fund from his portfolio of hedge funds, the FOF history is not influenced and the instant history bias will be absent; therefore, survivorship bias is less critical in FOFs than in individual hedge funds (Fung and Hsieh (2000)).

Traditional approaches to market timing may be unable to deal with hedge fund returns because of the dynamic trading strategies they use. However, using FOF active indices solves the problem. The usual management fee of FOFs is 1 percent to 2 percent, and the performance fee is on average 10 to 20 percent of capital appreciation. Some FOFs have hurdle rates (if the fund does not achieve returns above a proxy, the manager does not receive his incentive fee), or high watermarks (if returns are negative, the manager only receives the incentive once he passes the proxy). Moreover, some FOFs may have lock-up periods of up to two years and require advance notice regarding redemption, making market timing difficult for investors. This allows the FOF manager to protect himself from any massive withdrawals, and at the same time permits the manager to execute his strategies. Fothergill and Coke (2001) and Ineichen (2002) report that the greater majority of FOF managers offer monthly redemptions to investors. Using TASS data they find that 88 percent of FOFs have monthly redemptions, 9 percent quarterly redemptions, and the remaining 3 percent vary between semi-annually, annually, and weekly. In case of catastrophic events, some FOFs may even refuse to pay redemptions to investors. When using the ZCM database we find that of the live funds, 139 FOFs have quarterly redemptions, 123 monthly, 68 annually, and 23 semi-annually.

Market timing is a scientific method of forecasting the direction of the stock market; selection is the prediction of hedge fund movement. Selective managers, commonly known as micro forecasters, must profit from the trend. Market timers, or macro forecasters, must decide when to invest.

Jensen's (1968) test of micro forecasting and the Treynor and Mazuy (1966) (TM) and Henriksson and Merton (1981) (HM) tests of macro forecasting infer that both models perform well with and without adjustment for estimation risks. The use of conditional measures for the Jensen, TM, and HM models applies to a majority of FOFs since they have monthly, quarterly, semi-annual or annual redemptions with a 30-, 60- or 90-day period notice. However, it is common knowledge that FOF managers have contractual agreements with the hedge fund managers they invest in and the FOF managers are not subject to any type of lock-up periods, redemption periods and do not require written advance notice to redeem from the hedge funds in a majority of cases.

To better capture the alpha of FOFs, conditional measures are used that account for the risk and expected returns that continually change with the conditions of the economy and with the dynamic strategies used by hedge funds. Traditional and unconditional measures of performance do not take into consideration expected returns when the factors influencing market returns are changing. Ferson and Schadt (1996) developed a conditional model that corrects for the problem of risk and future returns when economic and market conditions change, thereby providing a better measure of the FOF's performance and its market timing ability.

The conditional approach implies that the strategy followed by the FOF manager can be reproduced. In other words, FOF managers who can efficiently process a 'greater' amount of public information than is usually available will possess superior market timing skills. By using lagged instruments to depict public information, such as the MSCI World Index lagged monthly dividend yields and the lagged US 30-day T-bill rate, FOF managers who add to or remove hedge funds from their portfolio using "systematic trading" will not be able to outperform the various FOF benchmarks. This effect will be picked up by the conditional models.

Conditional measures increase the hurdle rate of FOF managers looking for abnormal positive performance, since they receive no acknowledgment for using publicly available information. This chapter demonstrates that using conditional measures renders the performance of FOFs more precise during the investigation period. The results show that conditional alpha and beta provide better betas on average, which leads to better alphas (the essence of conditioning). The conditional models make use of time varying betas vis-à-vis publicly available information, since FOF managers act in response by frequently shifting their portfolio alphas and betas due to diverse economic and market conditions as well as market data.

As each FOF benchmark is examined, the adjusted R^2 varies along with the levels of alpha using the Jensen, TM, and HM models. Since no universal index for hedge funds and FOFs exists, FOFs are compared to various active FOF indices. This chapter aims to provide a selection tool to distinguish between good and bad FOFs.

A recent study suggested unifying all the hedge fund indices to create a universal index (Martellini and Amenc (2002)). This idea may not be feasible, however, because some hedge funds do not report to any database vendors. The consensus among past studies is that the majority of mutual fund managers have been poor market timers. But does this also apply to FOF managers as well? Can FOF managers select the best hedge funds and add alpha? Can FOF managers time when to be in the different hedge fund strategies?

This chapter is organized as follows. The next section presents the literature review followed by a description of the various models. Following this, we describe the data and methodologies used. We then present our empirical results and we analyze the results. The final section summarizes the essay and provides concluding remarks.

LITERATURE REVIEW

The benefits of diversifying traditional stock and bond portfolios with FOFs are well documented (Fung and Hsieh (1999, 2002); Schneeweis and Spurgin (1998a); deBrouwer (2001); Karavas (2000); Edwards and Caglayan (2001a); Fung and Hsieh (2002); Gregoriou and Rouah (2002); Ineichen (2001); Sharpe (1999); Fothergill and Coke (2002)). FOFs provide a better risk/return trade-off with reduced volatility and may provide higher returns than bond and equity mutual funds (Diz (2001)). Furthermore, the low correlation of FOFs to traditional markets provides investors with added value, especially in down markets (see Schneeweis and Spurgin (1998b); Liang (1999); Gregoriou (2000); Fung and Hsieh (1997); Agarwal and Naik (2000b)).

Investors now possess an overabundance of FOF managers available from database vendors such as ZCM (previously known as MAR), Hedge Fund Research (HFR) and Altvest. However, for academic studies TASS and Zurich contain the highest number of dead funds making them ideal for academic studies.

HFR, TASS and ZCM are database vendors that receive data from hedge funds and FOFs on a monthly basis, net of all fees. Hedge fund databases contain live hedge funds; dead funds must be requested separately. There is an approximate overlap of 40 percent and 28 percent of hedge funds, respectively, between HFR and TASS databases. Liang (2000) found 465 common funds between the HFR (1,162) and TASS (1,627) databases. Upon further examination, Liang (1999) observed that hedge fund returns are positively correlated with incentive fees, assets under management, and lock-up periods.

A description of hedge fund classifications is displayed in Table 3.1. Correlations for the indices used are displayed in Table 3.2. The approximate overlap of FOFs among the three indices is around 30 percent.

Since the hedge fund industry is considered opaque, experienced FOF managers who have a competitive information advantage will probably create superior and optimal FOFs (Ineichen (2002)). The notion that FOF managers can alter portfolio allocations frequently to ensure that hedge fund managers follow their strategy may possibly increase returns (Sharpe (1999)).

Table 3.1
Definition of Hedge Fund Styles Found in the Zurich/LaPorte Database

Global International	Manager pays attention to economic changes around the world (except in the U.S.)
Market Neutral	Half long/half short manager attempts to lock out or neutralize risk
Global Macro	Opportunistic trading manager who profits from changes in global economies, typically based on major interest rate shifts
Short Sellers	Manager takes a position that stock prices will go down. Used as a hedge for short-only portfolios
Long Only	Manager takes a position that stock prices will go up
Event Driven	Manager focuses on securities of companies in reorganization and bankruptcy, ranging from senior-secured debt to common stock
Fund of Funds	Capital is allocated among a number of hedge funds
Global Emerging	Manager invests in less mature financial markets. Because shorting is not permitted in many emerging markets, managers must go to cash or other markets when evaluations make being long unattractive
Global Established	Manager focuses on opportunities in established markets such as the U.S., Europe and Japan
Sector	Follows specific economic sectors and/or industries. Managers can use a wide range of methodologies

Source: Ackermann, McEnally and Ravenscraft (1999, p. 843) and www.marhedge.com.

Table 3.2
Correlation Matrix of FOF Indices vs. Market Indices, 1993-2001

Market Indices	*HFR*	*ZCM*	*ALTVEST*
S&P 500 index	0.51	0.56	0.57
MSCI World index	0.59	0.59	0.62
U.S. Salomon Government Bond Index	0.03	0.11	-0.11
DJIA	0.43	0.50	0.43
NASDAQ	0.64	0.59	0.82
RUSSELL 2000	0.68	0.70	0.83
HFR	×		
ZCM	0.93	×	
ALTVEST	0.81	0.75	×

Self-explanatory descriptive statistics for the three FOF indices used in this chapter are presented in Tables 3.3, while Table 3.4 displays the number of FOFs in each of the three indices.

Table 3.3
Descriptive Statistics of FOF Indices vs. Various Benchmarks, 1993-2001

Measure	*HFR*	*ZCM*	*ALTVEST*	*S&P 500*	*MSCI WORLD*	*US Salomon Government Bond Index*
Annualized Arithmetic Standard Deviation (%)	6.65	5.09	9.00	13.80	14.58	4.21
Maximum Drawdown (%)	13.08	7.04	8.93	33.83	30.49	5.33
Compounded Return (%)	131.12	143.41	405.83	137.55	213.70	85.32
Annualized Arithmetic Sharpe Ratio	0.80	1.14	1.59	0.46	0.66	0.64
High Period Return (%)	6.85	4.50	11.54	9.06	9.78	4.07
Low Period Return (%)	-7.47	-6.40	-5.92	-13.32	-14.46	-2.53
Percentages of Periods with a Gain (%)	67.59	77.78	76.85	63.89	65.74	71.30
Average Gain in a Gain Period (%)	1.76	1.38	2.48	3.27	3.58	1.15
Average Loss in a Losing Period (%)	-1.22	-1.05	-1.57	-3.34	-3.50	-0.83

Table 3.4
Number of Live FOFs in Hedge Fund Databases (Cumulative)

Year	*HFR*	*ZCM*	*ALTVEST*
1993	72	57	37
1994	88	80	42
1995	113	115	56
1996	138	142	87
1997	161	182	116
1998	194	217	165
1999	230	255	205
2000	256	300	225
2001	250	338	326

While almost 60 percent of mutual funds have R^2 above 75 percent with the S&P 500 index, hedge funds and FOFs on average have an R^2 of 53 percent and 32 percent, respectively (Ineichen (2002)). The dispersion of FOFs has increased on the downside during the latter half of the 1990s because of the higher volatility and turbulence in global markets. Unfortunately, institutional investors with no expertise in selecting hedge funds often choose the most established and well-known FOF managers, rather than relying on research.

The market timing and security selection of hedge funds is discussed in Gregoriou, Rouah and Sedzro (2002) using the TM model and a modified version. They observe that the majority of hedge fund managers possess superior security selection abilities and poor market timing skills when using large cap indices, but excellent market timing and selection skills when using small-cap indices.

Their data set contained 941 live hedge funds and 1,196 defunct funds classified by investment style. Both models displayed negative market timing skills similar to the results found in mutual fund studies. Gregoriou, Rouah and Sedzro (2002) used passive indices and the results may have been less robust. Likewise, the numerous biases inherent in hedge funds create problems when interpreting the data (Edwards and Caglayan (2001a), Liang (2000), Fung and Hsieh (2000)).

Hedge fund managers often use leverage to enhance portfolio returns. On average, hedge funds with very high levels of leverage tend to die faster (Gregoriou (2002) and Amin and Kat (2002a)). To prevent investors from being deceived by high alpha values, which are magnified as a result of leverage, the information ratio (alpha divided by the standard deviation) is frequently used to provide a more precise picture.

Research on market timing and security selection in the hedge fund literature is sparse. But academic studies on mutual funds conclude there is a negative correlation between market timing skills (often negative) and security selection abilities (Kon and Chen (1979), Henriksson and Merton (1981), Merton (1981), Henriksson (1984), Chang and Lewellen (1985), Lee and Rahman (1990) and Jagannathan and Korajczyk (1986)). However, Lehman and Modest (1987), Lee and Rahman (1990), Cumby and Glen (1990), Grinblatt and Titman (1994), and Janjigian and Bello (1997) found evidence of good market timing skills and superior security selection abilities in mutual funds.

According to Jagannathan and Korajczyk (1986), if a portfolio has a $\beta > 1$ than the market, security selection will be biased downward and market timing upward. The reverse is true if the portfolio has $\beta < 1$. Therefore, market timing exhibits positive correlation with beta, since beta increases with the amount of leverage used by the hedge fund. In many cases, varying the beta β_2 suggests that the model is misspecified, especially if the beta is constantly changing. This could be the result of misspecification of the market portfolio, or from neglecting to include certain factors in the model (Henriksson (1984)).

Since FOFs receive cash inflows and have lock-up periods, they are not affected by cash outflows, similarly to pension funds, which receive large chunks of money that cause no shifts in the distribution (Ferson, Christopherson and Glassman (1998)). But constant inflows and outflows of money in mutual funds cause a shift in their normal distribution (Ferson, Becker, Myers and Schill (1999), Sirri and Tufano (1993) and Zhang (1996)).

On the issue of performance, Brown, Goetzmann, and Ibbotson (1999) observed that during 1989-1995, hedge funds did not provide performance persistence. However, their study did not have the advantage of a large monthly database and was based on yearly hand-collected data, which resulted in less than robust results. More recently, Edwards and Caglayan (2001a) found evidence of performance persistence among the best-performing hedge funds, and even among some poorer-performing ones, which can be partly explained by higher incentive fees.

Numerous studies have reviewed the performance persistence of hedge funds (Brorsen and Harri (1998); Agarwal and Naik (2000c); Ackermann, Ravenscraft and McEnally (1999); Brown, Goetzmann and Ibbotson (1999); Schneeweis (1998); Asness, Krail and Liew (2001)), but their results are contingent on the database and examination period used in the analysis (Liang (2000)). Agarwal and Naik (2000c) find that the level of persistence decreases as they move from quarterly to yearly returns regardless of the time frame. They find no evidence of persistence when using annual returns with a multi-period framework. But there are a few good managers who consistently perform well for long periods of time, which indicates the importance of hedge fund manager selection. Persistence seems to be unrelated to whether the fund takes directional bets.

This is consistent with the finding that hedge fund managers regularly modify the weights of the assets comprising their portfolios (Fung and

Hsieh (1997), Brown Goetzmann and Ibbotson (1999) and Brown, Goetzmann and Park (2000)). Fung and Hsieh (1997) argue that a hedge fund manager's returns usually have three components (1) the asset categories the manager invests in (2) the hedge fund strategy (3) the use of leverage. Mutual fund managers, however, use only the first two.

Bollen and Busse (2001) and Goetzmann, Ingersoll, and Ivkovic (2000) report that using monthly data may distort the market timing skills of active managers, since portfolio turnover occurs more frequently than just monthly. Also, hedge fund managers commonly turn over entire portfolios in one month. Unfortunately, hedge fund database vendors only supply monthly data. There are, however, a handful of hedge funds and FOFs that provide daily liquidity, for example, Deutsche Asset Management, which is touted as the largest FOF with assets over $5 billion.

MODELS OF MARKET TIMING AND SECURITY SELECTION

We are using an international asset pricing model because FOFs are globally diversified and have different hedge fund managers using a broad range of strategies investing in many countries as well as emerging market economies (Dahlquist and Harvey (2001)). The FOF index is used as the market in order to evaluate this within the context of a tracking error framework; as variables, we use MSCI world dividend yield and the 30-day U.S. T-bill rate. The MSCI world dividend yield and the 30-day U.S. T-bill rate represent public information available to FOF managers and thus the variables are qualified to act as instruments for hedge fund markets.

Considering the dynamic nature of their trading strategies reflected in the continuous rebalancing of their portfolios, it is tricky to measure market timing when using hedge funds. Further, using conditional HM and TM models will require the addition of other factors to lend power to these tests. In principle, one can do this using the framework proposed by Ferson and Warther (1996) and Ferson and Schadt (1996).

When examining FOF performance, it is common to evaluate the manager's skill with regard to a market proxy. Tracking error represents the annual standard deviation of the differences in the returns between the FOF and the FOF indices (the proxy) and measures the extent by which the returns of the FOF diverge from those of the proxy as a result of the investment decisions made by the FOF manager. Therefore, if a FOF manager is not able to outperform the FOF indices, it may perhaps be due to an overweighting, underweighting, or even due to the selection of underlying hedge fund managers, which plays an important role in the tracking error framework. The effect of tracking error will be reduced in the conditional models and will present a more accurate picture of the FOF manager's skill and timing ability.

Unconditional Jensen's Alpha

Many studies use the capital asset pricing model (CAPM) developed by Sharpe (1964) and Lintner (1965) and Jensen (1968) proposed a measure alpha of average performance to assess a portfolio manager's forecasting skills. Fama (1972) posited that the performance of portfolio managers can be split into two essential parts: selection and market timing. Alpha, the traditional measure of relative performance, does not consider market timing. Therefore, CAPM predicts that the intercept term is zero when there are no superior returns. Furthermore, CAPM postulates that the returns of a fund follow a normal distribution, which is not true for hedge funds and FOFs, as they exhibit non-linear returns.

Portfolio returns can be represented as linear functions of systematic risk, the realized returns on the market portfolio, the risk-free rate, and a random error. Jensen's (1968) alpha measures the market risk-adjusted excess rate of return (above the risk free rate) against the excess rate of return on the market and is calculated as the intercept of the unconditional regression model in Equation (1):

$$r_{pt} - r_{ft} = \alpha_p + \beta_i (r_{mt} - r_{ft}) + \varepsilon_{pt} , \qquad (1)$$

where $r_{pt} - r_{ft}$ is the excess rate of return on portfolio p during period t over the 30-day U.S. T-bill rate (or the risk free rate of return), $r_{mt} - r_{ft}$ is the excess return on the benchmark (FOF Index) during period t, α_p is the unconditional measure of the selection abilities, β_i is the unconditional beta and ε_{pt} is the random error term for FOF p in period *t* (unsystematic risk in portfolio). Positive and statistically significant values represent superior FOF performance.

Market timing and selection must be measured concurrently, because focusing merely on market timing may cause bias in measuring alpha (see Grinblatt and Titman 1989)). Jensen's measure is imprecise if the fund manager is a market timer. Market timing expresses the FOF manager's ability to time the allocation between hedge funds and cash to capture gains in up markets and avoid losses in down markets. To consider the effect of market timing ability, we use the TM and HM models.

Conditional Jensen Model

If FOF managers dynamically use market timing, Jensen's model may lead to unreliable results. Since beta and returns are constantly changing, many studies propose using conditional performance measures (Ferson and Warther (1996), Ferson and Schadt (1996), Harvey and Graham (1995), and Chen and Knez (1996)). We adopt Ferson and Schadt's (1996) and Ferson and Warter's (1996) techniques and measure the condition of the market where the risk of a portfolio must be related to market indicators. For instance, MSCI world dividend yield and short-term 30-day U.S. T-bill rate lagged one period when estimating performance. We employ a lagged model because we are interested in the ability of FOF managers to select the best performing hedge funds on a predictive basis. In other words, if the FOF manger adjusts the market betas in response to only public information (such as the dividend yield and the T-bill rate), he will likely not possess market timing ability, which is the essence conditioning.

We use the same variables but measure the T-bill yield at the start of the period. The conditional Jensen model is (Equation 2):

$$r_{pt} - r_{ft} = \alpha_{cp} + \beta_{0p}(r_{mt} - r_{ft}) + \beta_{1p}[MSCI_{t-1}(r_{mt} - r_{ft})] + \beta_{2p}[TB_{t-1}(r_{mt} - r_{ft})] + \tag{2}$$

where α_{cp} is the conditional performance measure, β_{0p} is the conditional beta, and β_{1p} and β_{2p} measure the rate at which the conditional beta differs when compared to the MSCI world dividend yield and the 30-day U.S. T-bill rate lagged one period. $MSCI_{t-1}$ is the MSCI monthly dividend yield as of the start of the period t and TB_{t-1} is the (observable) 30-day U.S. T-bill rate also lagged one period.

Unconditional Treynor-Mazuy Model

The Treynor-Mazuy (1966) model claims that if managers can successfully forecast market returns, they would purchase larger proportions of the market portfolio in an up market smaller proportions during a down market. Since the betas of hedge fund managers constantly change and their portfolio weights are not usually known (Brown, Goetzmann and Ibbotson (1999)), the TM model may prove ideal for examining market timing performance.

However, identifying an appropriate benchmark model is difficult because hedge fund managers trade frequently and use dynamic strategies and a variety of derivative instruments. Hedge funds also exhibit nonlinear exposures to standard asset markets as well as options like returns (Agarwal and Naik (2000a)). The unconditional regression TM is (Equation 3):

$$r_{pt} - r_{ft} = \alpha_p + \beta_1 (r_{mt} - r_{ft}) + \beta_2 (r_{mt} - r_{ft})^2 + \varepsilon_{pt}, \quad (3)$$

where

t	=	time period,
r_{pt}	=	rate of return on FOF p during period t,
r_{ft}	=	risk free rate (30-day U.S. T-bill rate)
r_{mt}	=	return on the market index (FOF Index) during period t,
α_p	=	estimated of selection performance of the FOF manager,
β_1	=	estimate of systematic risk,
β_i	=	estimate of market timing performance, and
ε_{pt}	=	random error term for FOF p in period t (unsystematic risk in portfolio).

The TM model examines the likelihood of these inherent biases, and essentially analyzes the sources of FOF performance. Portfolio performance evaluation in the TM model has been controversial. Admati et al. (1986) first explained that, under certain conditions, the TM model satisfactorily measured the market timing ability of fund managers. Dellva, DeMaskey and Smith (2001) argue that a positive value of β_2 represents superior market timing ability, because the returns of the portfolio are more responsive to positive rather than to negative returns. If no market timing is found, then β_2 =0, while a negative value of β_2 represents inferior market timing.

Indeed, since $r_{mt}^2 > 0$, a positive value of β_2 in equation (1) ensures that r_{pt} will not substantially decrease when $r_{mt} < 0$. Conversely, when β_2 <0, r_{pt} will decrease faster than when $\beta_2 \geq 0$. Therefore, in the TM model, the negative effect of market downturns on the FOF portfolio returns is mitigated in FOF managers with superior market timing and amplified in those with inferior market timing. This would cause the FOF to exhibit convex properties as a function of the market return displayed by the coefficient of the quadratic term β_2 in Equation (3).

The TM model yields a greater proportion of negative market timing along with a negative correlation between market timing and security selection, as noted by Kon and Chen (1979) and Chang and Lewellen (1985). Lehman and Modest (1987), Grinblatt and Titman (1989) and Elton et al. (1993) find that U.S. equity mutual fund performance varies depending on the benchmark used.

Henriksson-Merton Unconditional Model

Henriksson and Merton (1981) (HM) derived a non-parametric and a parametric test of forecasting ability frequently referred to as the dual beta model. This model takes into account that forecasting skills are different for up markets than for down markets. HM developed the model by fitting two linear regressions to the data points using up markets when the FOF outperforms the T-bill rate and in down markets when it underperforms the T-bill rate. The regression model is:

$$r_{pt} - r_{ft} = \alpha_p + \beta_{1p}(r_{mt} - r_{ft}) + \beta_{2p}[D(r_{mt} - r_{ft})] + \varepsilon_{pt}\,, \qquad (4)$$

where $r_{pt} - r_{ft}$ is the excess return of the portfolio, D is a dummy variable (equal to 1 if the market return exceeds the risk-free rate), and ε is the random error term, having a value of –1 for down market returns $(r_{mt} < r_{ft})$ or zero for up market return $(r_{mt} \geq r_{ft})$.

The model considers that the alpha (α_p) is the measure of selection (risk-adjusted return), is not influenced by either up or down markets. The β_{1p} term is the systematic risk of the fund and the slope β_{2p} is the measure of market timing ability that will change in up or down markets.

The HM model may be considered superior because it assumes that forecasters can forecast if market returns surpass the risk-free rate.

Conditional TM Model

Ferson and Schadt (1996) demonstrate that a conditional performance evaluation can be constructed on the similar theoretical premise as the regular models and develop conditional performance measures within a CAPM and arbitrage pricing theory (APT) framework. When using conditional performance measures, they find that the average fund performance becomes marginally positive, while most studies find negative average performance. Their studies suggest that both the benchmark portfolio and the performance measure can affect hedge fund performance. The conditional models include the time variation in the FOF's beta, which will differ with a certain number of market variables (indicators). The following is the conditional regression version of the TM market timing model (Equation 5):

$$r_{pt} - r_{ft} = \alpha_p + \beta_{0p}(r_{mt} - r_{ft}) + \beta_{1p}[MSCI_{t-1}(r_{mt} - r_{ft})] + \beta_{2p}[TB_{t-1}(r_{mt} - r_{ft})] + \gamma_p(r_{mt} - r_{ft})^2 + \varepsilon_{pt}, \quad (5)$$

where α_p is the conditional measure of performance, β_{0p} is the conditional beta, β_{1p} and β_{2p} measure how the conditional beta varies with respect to the MSCI world dividend yield and 30-day US T-bill rate (both lagged) and γ_p is the market-timing coefficient.

The coefficient measure is the sensitivity of the FOF's beta to any private market timing ability beyond the information about the future shape of the market return contained in the MSCI world dividend yield and the T-bill rate lagged variables. Therefore, the conditional market-timing models attempt to differentiate between predictive market timing based exclusively on public data and predictive market timing that is in fact better than public data. In other words, the conditional models raise the hurdle bar for the FOF manager and will reveal whether he is good at market timing.

The coefficients β_{1p} and β_{2p} determine how sensitive the beta is with regard to better interpretation of information or data by the FOF manager regarding the outlook of the market performance inherent in the MSCI world dividend yield and the T-bill rate lagged variables.

Conditional Henriksson-Merton Model

The same is used for the conditional HM model using the regression (Equation 6):

$$r_{pt} - r_{ft} = \alpha_p + \beta_{0p}(r_{mt} - r_{ft}) + \beta_{1p}[MSCI_{t-1}(r_{mt} - r_{ft})] + \beta_{2p}[TB_{t-1}(r_{mt} - r_{ft})] + \gamma_p(r_{mt} - r_{ft})^* + \beta^*_{1p}[MSCI_{t-1}(r_{mt} - r_{ft})^*] + \beta^*_{2p}[TB_{t-1}(r_{mt} - r_{ft})^*] + \varepsilon_{pt}, \quad (6)$$

where $(r_{mt} - r_{ft})^*$ is the return of the FOF index less the risk-free rate multiplied by a dummy variable for returns greater than zero against the excess return on the FOF index and the conditional mean of the excess return identified as $(r_{mt} - r_{ft})^*$. A linear regression was subsequently performed on the excess returns of the various FOF indices on $MSCI_{t-1}$ and TB_{t-1}, thus providing an estimated value for the conditional mean.

The market timing coefficient, γ_p, is the most important (i.e., the difference between the up and down market conditional beta).

DATA AND METHODOLOGY

We adopt the methodology of Dellva, DeMaskey, and Smith (2001), Ferson and Schadt (1996), and Ferson and Warther (1996) and apply it to FOF data. Our sample is January 1993-December 2001, a time frame that encompasses up and down markets along with extreme market movements. The data consist of 227 live and 210 dead offshore and onshore FOFs that reported monthly results (net of all fees) to ZCM.

We only consider funds with a minimum of 24 months of performance history for the entire period because a 36-month minimum results in the exclusion of many non-surviving funds. This can cause upward bias in the performance returns because of survivorship and potential instant history biases (Edwards and Cagalyan (2001a)). Since we use cross-sectional analysis, the number of live and dead funds vary during the sub-periods.

Due to the global diversification nature of funds of hedge funds, an international asset pricing model is used to measure performance as previous studies have shown (Dahlquist and Harvey (2001)). We use the lagged MSCI monthly dividend yields and the lagged U.S. 30-day T-bill rate. If we were examining pure hedge funds, the S&P 500 monthly dividend yield would have been preferred (Edwards and Caglayan (2001a)). In all our regression models, we use White's (1980) correction to test for heteroskedasticity and no evidence was found at all confidence levels.

Defunct funds are included to eliminate survivorship bias. Selection bias remains, however, because the hedge fund industry is essentially unregulated and managers report fund information only voluntarily. Consequently, funds tend to be brought into databases with return history, which has two implications. First, a fund might appear in a database because a manager has chosen to report a good track record, thereby introducing self-selection bias. Secondly, there is the possibility of backfill bias, which occurs if database vendors backfill a hedge fund's performance when a new fund is added instead of only including its returns going forward. This overstates index performance since inclusion in the index is voluntary and thus funds will only be added after very good past performance. For each rolling 5-year period the number of funds vary and are indicated by the number of alphas at the top of each table.

Three benchmarks are used to evaluate the selection and market timing of FOFs. Choosing a suitable benchmark is critical in evaluating hedge fund manager performance (Fung and Hsieh (1997, 2002)), Gregoriou, Rouah, and Sedzro (2002), Brown, Goetzmann, and Park (2001), Edwards and Caglayan (2001a), and Agarwal and Naik (2001b). We use the FOF indices as benchmarks because FOF managers need to outperform their peers rather traditional and passive benchmarks (Brown, Goetzmann, and Park (2001), Fung and Hsieh (1997, 2002), and Rostron and Colvin (1999)). Sharpe (1999) also agrees that manager skill is difficult to measure because alternative benchmarks to FOF strategies do not exist. He recommends that FOFs use manager universe comparisons to verify some form of manager skill comparison. Fung and Hsieh (2002) discovered that FOF indices do not suffer from spurious biases that can emanate from impractical asset allocation design. Furthermore, the low attrition rate in FOFs implies that survivorship bias will not affect our results (Fung and Hsieh (1997)).

For our purposes, the only available FOF indices used as benchmarks were the following: the HFR FOF Index, the ALTVEST FOF Index, and the ZCM FOF Index. The other database that contained funds of hedge funds as a classification was the Van Hedge database; however, it is a restricted database and their data of FOFs begins in 1995. ALTVEST, HFR, and ZCM contain the classification for our period of analysis and are equally weighted indices.

EMPIRICAL RESULTS

The results for Jensen's unconditional model of measuring performance for January 1993-December 2001 are shown in Table 3.5. The results in all of the tables are calculated by running a separate regression for each individual FOF and then taking the average.

We fit one model to the FOF classification as defined in Tables 3.5, 3.6, and 3.7 using the HFR, Altvest, and ZCM indices as benchmarks, while considering risk-adjusted returns. To measure the performance, the average positive and negative alphas for all FOFs are disclosed using one-tailed tests at 1 percent, 5 percent, and 10 percent levels. The average R^2 values are also displayed for the Jensen, TM, and HM models Tables 3.5-3.7.

When comparing the conditional and unconditional models, a lower number of significant positive and negative alphas are found and a lower number of market timing coefficients in all the conditional models. The adjusted R^2s are higher in all the conditional models, due to the variation of FOF betas and market returns. The conditional models are able to capture the variation as a result of the variables used (dividend yield and T-bill rate).

Table 3.5 displays the descriptive results of the statistical performance measures of the unconditional Jensen model. The average alpha is favorable (positive) and statistically significant for HFR. However, the average alphas are unfavorable and statistically significant when using Altvest and ZCM. These results show that FOF managers can outperform the HFR benchmark, but cannot beat the Altvest and ZCM benchmarks.

It is found that the correlation between ZCM and Altvest is the lowest (Table 3.2) and therefore the results will differ more than between HFR and ZCM, which have the highest correlation.

Table 3.6 displays the result of the unconditional TM model. The average alpha is favorable and statistically significant using HFR, but unfavorable (negative) and statistically significant when using Altvest and ZCM. When investigating the average market timing performance, it is found that the results are unfavorable and statistically insignificant with the HFR benchmark and unfavorable and statistically significant with the Altvest benchmark, but favorable and statistically significant with the ZCM benchmark.

Table 3.5
Summary Descriptive Statistics Following Unconditional Jensen Model, 1993-2001

HFR FOF INDEX	
Parameter	*Mean*
Alpha t_α	0.0747
	(0.0181)*
Beta Beta $t_{\beta 1}$	0.9252
	(<.0001)**
R^{2-}Adjusted	0.4328
	(<.0001)**

ALTVEST FOF INDEX	
Parameter	*Mean*
Alpha Beta t_α	-0.2944
	(<.0001)**
Beta Beta $t_{\beta 1}$	0.5960
	(<.0001)**
R^{2-}Adjusted	0.3588
	(<.0001)**

ZCM FOF INDEX	
Parameter	*Mean*
Alpha t_α	-0.0899
	(0.0117)*
Beta $t_{\beta 1}$	1.224
	(<.0001)**
R^{2-}Adjusted	0.4146
	(<.0001)**

Table 3.6
Summary Descriptive Statistics Following Unconditional TM Model, 1993-2001

HFR FOF INDEX

Parameter	*Mean*
Alpha t_α	0.0782
	(0.0078)**
Beta $t_{\beta 1}$	0.9393
	(<.0001)**
Beta $t_{\beta 2}$ (Timing coeff.)	-0.0106
	(0.0765)
R^2-Adjusted	0.4778
	(<.0001)**

ALTVEST FOF INDEX

Parameter	*Mean*
Alpha t_α	-0.2232
	(<.0001)**
Beta $t_{\beta 1}$	0.6354
	(<.0001)**
Beta $t_{\beta 2}$ (Timing coeff.)	-0.0167
	(.0011)**
R^2-Adjusted	0.3989
	(<.0001)**

ZCM FOF INDEX

Parameter	*Mean*
Alpha t_α	-0.1544
	(<.0001)**
Beta $t_{\beta 1}$	1.2534
	(<.0001)**
Beta $t_{\beta 2}$ (Timing coeff.)	0.0185
	(0.0419)*
R^2-Adjusted	0.4523
	(<.0001)**

Table 3.7 introduces the unconditional HM model. The average alpha using HFR is favorable but not significant. Both Altvest and ZCM display unfavorable average alphas and are significant. The market timing performance using HFR is favorable but statistically insignificant, whereas Altvest is negative and significant. With ZCM, the performance is positive and significant. Here, FOF managers display good market timing skills on average and can outperform the ZCM benchmark.

Table 3.7
Summary Descriptive Statistics Following Unconditional HM Model, 1993-2001

HFR FOF INDEX	
Parameter	*Mean*
Alpha t_α	0.0037
	(0.9405)
Beta $t_{\beta 1}$	0.8985
	(<.0001)**
Beta $t_{\beta 2}$ (Timing Coeff.)	0.1394
	(0.0558)
R^2-Adjusted	0.4477
	(<.0001)**
ALTVEST FOF INDEX	
Parameter	*Mean*
Alpha t_α	-0.1963
	(.0004)**
Beta $t_{\beta 1}$	0.6206
	(<.0001)**
Beta $t_{\beta 2}$ (Timing Coeff.)	0.1954
	(0.0229)*
R^2-Adjusted	0.3767
	(<.0001)**
ZCM FOF INDEX	
Parameter	*Mean*
Alpha t_α	-0.1982
	(0.0008)**
Beta $t_{\beta 1}$	1.1817
	(<.0001)**
Beta $t_{\beta 2}$ (Timing Coeff.)	0.2098
	(0.0206)*
R^2-Adjusted	0.4433
	(<.0001)**

Table 3.8
Summary Descriptive Statistics Following Ferson and Schadt (1996) Conditional Jensen's Model, 1993-2001

HFR FOF INDEX

Parameter	*Mean*
Alpha t_α	0.0615
	(.0549)
Beta $t_{\beta 0}$	0.7050
	(.0167)*
Beta $t_{\beta 1}$	0.0146
	(.9912)
Beta $t_{\beta 2}$	0.4433
	(.4013)
R^2-Adjusted	0.4912
	(<.0001)**

ALTVEST FOF INDEX

Parameter	*Mean*
Alpha t_α	-0.3135
	(<.0001)**
Beta $t_{\beta 0}$	0.4593
	(.0166)*
Beta $t_{\beta 1}$	0.5898
	(.5732)
Beta $t_{\beta 2}$	0.0039
	(.9911)
R^2-Adjusted	0.4129
	(<.0001)**

ZCM FOF INDEX

Parameter	*Mean*
Alpha t_α	-0.1037
	(.0039)**
Beta $t_{\beta 0}$	1.7050
	(<.0001)**
Beta $t_{\beta 1}$	-5.3725
	(.0060)**
Beta $t_{\beta 2}$	0.4171
	(.4564)
R^2-Adjusted	0.4689
	(<.0001)**

Table 3.8 shows the first conditional model. Using HFR produces a favorable average alpha that is not significant, while using Altvest and ZCM produces negative and significant average alphas. The dividend yield and

T-bill rate are favorable but not significant when using HFR, and not favorable and not significant when using Altvest, which does not explain FOF returns. ZCM produces negative and significant dividend yield, which explains FOF returns, but the coefficient on the T-bill rate is favorable and not significant.

Table 3.9 displays the conditional TM model and shows the average alphas are favorable and significant using HFR, but negative and significant with Altvest and ZCM. The dividend yield and the T-bill rate are not significant when using HFR and Altvest, which does not explain FOF returns. Lastly, when using ZCM, the dividend yield is negative and significant, which explains FOF returns, and the T-bill rate is positive but not significant. Market timing performance is both negative and significant when using HFR and Altvest, and positive but not significant with ZCM.

Table 3.10 displays the conditional HM model and shows that the average alphas are favorable and significant using HFR, but negative and significant with Altvest and ZCM. The table also shows that the dividend yield and the T-bill rate are not significant when using HFR, Altvest, and ZCM, which do not explain FOF returns.

Using the various FOF benchmarks has given us different results. This can be attributed to the fact that the Altvest index has a greater compounded return when compared to HFR and ZCM. When compared to HFR and ZCM, Altvest has the highest correlation with the Nasdaq and Russell 2000 indices. This may be due to the FOFs managers in the Altvest index concentrating on selecting more technology and small cap individual hedge fund managers.

SUMMARY AND CONCLUSION

Using the various FOF benchmarks has given us different results. This can be attributed to the fact that the Altvest index has a greater compounded return when compared to HFR and ZCM. This may be due to the FOF managers in the Altvest index concentrating on selecting more technology and small cap individual hedge fund managers. When comparing the three databases, Altvest has the highest correlation with the Nasdaq and Russell 2000 indices. In many academic papers, the most frequently used databases are HFR, ZCM, and TASS; Altvest is seldom used.

Table 3.9
Summary Descriptive Statistics Following Ferson and Schadt (1996) Conditional TM Model, 1993-2001

HFR FOF INDEX

Parameter	*Mean*
Alpha t_α	0.0735
	(.0116)*
Beta $t_{\beta 0}$	0.7084
	(.0160)*
Beta $t_{\beta 1}$	0.0628
	(.9605)
Beta $t_{\beta 2}$	0.3876
	(.4617)
Gamma (Timing coeff.)	-0.0140
	(.0280)*
R^2 Adjusted	0.5279
	(<.0001)**

ALTVEST FOF INDEX

Parameter	*Mean*
Alpha t_α	-0.2423
	(<.0001)**
Beta $t_{\beta 0}$	0.5621
	(.0017)**
Beta $t_{\beta 1}$	0.0964
	(.9188)
Beta $t_{\beta 2}$	-0.0149
	(.9642)
Gamma (Timing Coeff.)	-0.0180
	(.0006)**
R^2 Adjusted	0.4437
	(<.0001)**

ZCM FOF INDEX

Parameter	*Mean*
Alpha t_α	-0.1576
	(<.0001)**
Beta $t_{\beta 0}$	1.8668
	(<.0001)**
Beta $t_{\beta 1}$	-5.1675
	(.0054)**
Beta $t_{\beta 2}$	-0.0059
	(.9913)
Gamma (Timing Coeff.)	0.0139
	(.1541)
R^2 Adjusted	0.5007
	(<.0001)**

Table 3.10
Summary Descriptive Statistics Following Ferson and Schadt (1996) Conditional HM Model, 1993-2001

HFR FOF INDEX

Parameter	*Mean*
Alpha t_{α}	0.0870
	(.0110*)
Beta $t_{\beta 0}$	1.7084
	(.0080)**
Beta $t_{\beta 1}$	-3.6347
	(.1782)
Beta $t_{\beta 2}$	-0.6921
	(.5214)
Beta $t_{\beta 1}$*	3.1257
	(.3411)
Beta $t_{\beta 2}$*	0.7578
	(.5862)
Gamma (Timing Coeff.)	-0.8612
	(.2679)
R^2 Adjusted	0.5673
	(<.0001)**

ALTVEST FOF INDEX

Parameter	*Mean*
Alpha t_{α}	-0.2247
	(<.0001)**
Beta $t_{\beta 0}$	1.3148
	(.0049)**
Beta $t_{\beta 1}$	-5.3970
	(.1393)
Beta $t_{\beta 2}$	0.3720
	(.7547)
Beta $t_{\beta 1}$*	5.5582
	(.1453)
Beta $t_{\beta 2}$*	-0.5108
	(.6709)
Gamma (Timing Coeff.)	-0.8161
	(.0994)
R^2 Adjusted	0.4729
	(.<0001)**

ZCM FOF INDEX

Parameter	*Mean*
Alpha t_{α}	-0.2197
	(<.0001)**
Beta $t_{\beta 0}$	2.1294
	(.0503)
Beta $t_{\beta 1}$	-4.1664
	(.3696)
Beta $t_{\beta 2}$	-0.8164
	(.6416)
Beta $t_{\beta 1}$*	-4.3903
	(.4148)
Beta $t_{\beta 2}$*	-0.2287
	(.9051)
Gamma (Timing Coeff.)	0.6653
	(.0569)
R^2 Adjusted	0.5364
	(<.0001)**

The selection and market timing performance of funds of hedge funds are examined using conditional and unconditional alphas and betas. The results suggest that conditional models as proposed by Ferson and Warther (1996) and Ferson and Schadt (1996) are preferred over unconditional models for estimating future returns.

It is concluded that conditioning the alphas and betas can offer a slightly improved perspective regarding the identification of superior FOF managers. This is confirmed by the higher R^2 values found in the conditional models, which render a more accurate picture of the market timing skills and selectivity of FOF managers.

Due to the problems of dynamic trading strategies and the public information used here, unconditional models indicate significant abnormal performance; thus, the FOF manager cannot be considered as possessing above average market timing skills. However, when using conditional models it is found that alphas, betas, and timing coefficients represent a more correct depiction than the unconditional models. We find that the alphas are higher and there is a greater number of insignificant market timing coefficients in the conditional models.

It seems that the chapter succeeds in presenting support for the better conditional models as opposed to the unconditional models as we originally claimed because abnormal performance disappears in the conditional models, as confirmed by Ferson and Schadt (1996) and Ferson and Warther (1996).

A possibility for further research could be to use TASS, HFR, Altvest, and the Barclay CTA databases and examine the different hedge fund and CTA classifications.

CHAPTER 4

Fund of Hedge Fund Performance Using Data Envelopment Analysis

INTRODUCTION

Much recent debate has centered on how to measure and evaluate the performance of hedge funds. The task is particularly difficult due to the lack of correlation between hedge funds and traditional stock and bond market indices. In the literature, we frequently observe hedge fund rankings displayed using measures such as the Sharpe ratio. But this may pose problems due to the option-like returns that hedge funds generate.

Numerous authors have also used linear multifactor models and passive indices to examine hedge fund performance (Gregoriou, Rouah, and Sedzro (2002), Edwards and Caglayan (2001)). However, as Brealey and Kaplanis (2001) note, there are problems inherent in using these types of traditional approaches in a world of non-normal returns. For example, because of their dynamic trading strategies, hedge funds do not have stable exposure to market factors over time.

We aim to eliminate the weaknesses posed by traditional measures by using Data Envelopment Analysis (DEA) models to identify and evaluate the performance and efficiency of hedge fund classifications. DEA permits us to evaluate and rank the efficiency of hedge funds in a risk-return framework without using indices.

We select the fund of hedge funds (FOF) classification because of its recent popularity and acceptance by institutional investors and pension funds for diversifying traditional stock and bond portfolios (Amenc and Martellini (2002)).

We find that many FOFs are inefficient when evaluated by basic DEA models. Having an alternative performance measure like DEA is important because it enables investors to potentially pinpoint the reasons behind a fund's poor performance, instead of just using benchmarks. Once the weaknesses are recognized, the fund can attempt to reach a score of 100 in the future. This is why we believe that using DEA as an alternative measure to select funds when building a hedge fund portfolio is optimal. Examining the performance of funds of hedge funds via DEA will allow us to identify and rank the efficient funds of hedge funds in a risk-return framework.

History of DEA

DEA is a mathematical evaluation or linear programming technique that measures the relative efficiency of decision-making units (DMUs) on the basis of observed data, and then presents an efficiency score as a single number between 0 and 100. An efficiency score of 100 refers to an efficient fund; a score of 0 means the fund is inefficient. DEA is a non-parametric technique. Its main benefit is that it identifies the best-performing fund and determines the relative efficiencies of a set of similar funds as well.

DEA, also called frontier analysis, was initially developed by Charnes, Cooper, and Rhodes (CCR) (1978). It was later adapted by Banker, Charnes, and Cooper (BCC) (1984), who expanded the Farrell (1957) technical measure of efficiency from a single-input, single-output process to a multiple-input, multiple-output process. The CCR and BCC models are the basic DEA models. They were originally developed for non-profit organizations. Later we discuss two more powerful DEA techniques, cross-evaluation and super-efficiency.

The non-linear nature of hedge fund strategies makes the application of DEA particularly pertinent. The power of DEA is in its ability to manage multiple inputs and outputs while not demanding a specific functional form for input and output relationships. The single measure of performance, which takes into account the multiple measurements of variables to estimate a fund's efficiency level, is particularly useful for evaluating FOFs.

The purpose of this chapter is to demonstrate that DEA can be used in the FOF selection process, either for stand-alone investments or for traditional stock, bond, or currency portfolios. We present a new approach for quantifying FOF management quality, using three DEA models comprised of multiple inputs and outputs to compute a measure of relative efficiency ranking for FOFs.

Overview of DEA

The first step in the DEA process is to distinguish an efficient frontier from the inputs and outputs identified by the use of Pareto optimality.[2] Pareto optimality means the best that can be attained without putting any group at a disadvantage. In other words, a group of funds becomes better off if an individual fund becomes better off and none become worse off.

DEA then calculates the efficiency score of each DMU relative to the efficiency frontier. In this chapter, the DMUs are the FOFs.

The efficiency frontier consists of the "best-performing" funds, *e.g.*, those with an efficiency score of 100. These funds are the most efficient at transforming the inputs into outputs (CCR (1981)). A best performance frontier charts the maximum or minimum level of output (input) produced for any assumed level of input (output). Outputs represent the degree to which the FOF's goal has been achieved.

Models must be cautiously selected based on the type of industry being examined. For example, will inputs or outputs be controlled, or not? Controlled inputs or outputs are units over which the organization has control and can change the amount of resources used. Uncontrolled variables are those the hedge fund does not control.

The use of proper input minimization and output maximization must also be thoroughly understood. The inputs and outputs used in the efficiency analysis are essential since they establish the grounds on which the efficiency of the funds is calculated.

The most extensively used DEA technique to measure efficiency takes the weighted sum of outputs and divides it by the weighted sum of inputs (this is also called the engineering ratio) (Golany and Roll (1994)). In its simplest form, DEA expresses the choice of the weights represented by a linear program by maximizing relative efficiency with a set of minimal weight constraints. CCR (1978) proposed reducing the multiple-input, multiple-output model to a ratio with a single virtual input and a single virtual output. This was done by estimating a set of weights depicting each unit in the most favorable position relative to other units.

Basic DEA

The main distinction between the two basic DEA models is that the BCC model uses varying returns to scale to examine the relative efficiency of units, while the CCR model uses constant returns to scale. The BCC model permits a greater amount of optimal solutions to be obtained. With the BCC model, the number of funds with an efficiency score of 100 will, on average, be higher than the CCR model. Choosing between these models requires insight into what the process will involve. For example, if the increase in inputs does not provide the same increase in outputs, then the variable returns to scale model should be used.

With small samples, DEA may produce biased results. To obtain robust results, it is normally accepted that a proper working sample should be about three times the number of input and output variables. DEA is not backed by a theoretical framework, but rather uses a comparative measure of relative performance framework.

Cross-Evaluation

The cross-evaluation, or cross-efficiency, model was developed by Sexton, Silkman, and Hogan (1986). It establishes the ranking procedure and computes the efficiency score of each unit *n* times using optimal weights measured by the linear programs.

Cross-evaluation is performed continually for each fund of hedge funds in our sample. The DEA method renders an ex post evaluation of a fund's efficiency and specifies the precise input-output relationship. This must be realized without an efficiency score greater than 100 when the coefficients are adapted to the funds in our sample. Efficiency scores, as they are relative to the other funds in the sample, are by no means absolute.

Super-Efficiency

Super-efficiency, another method to rank efficient units, was developed by Andersen and Petersen (1993). It is similar to the BCC model, but it excludes the fund under evaluation from the reference set. This method allows a highly efficient fund to attain an efficiency score greater than 100.

We noted that, since hedge funds and funds of hedge funds display non-linear characteristics, it is difficult to find appropriate active benchmarks (Gregoriou, Rouah, and Sedzro (2002); Agarwal and Naik (2001)). Joro and Na (2001) develop a mean-variance skewness framework to examine portfolio performance measurement, thereby surmounting the problems of the traditional capital asset pricing model (CAPM). For pension funds considering using FOFs as downside protection in bear markets, it is critical that a performance measure provide not only a precise measure of the fund's performance, but also an idea of the quality of its management with respect to certain criteria (variables such as inputs and outputs). Using certain variables in DEA may provide pension funds with a useful tool for screening and ranking funds hedge funds, not by historical returns, but by peer group appraisal.

LITERATURE REVIEW

DEA papers have been published in many sectors, and its use has often resulted in technical and efficiency improvements. DEA has also been used recently to evaluate the performance of mutual funds and to determine the most efficient (see, for example, Sedzro and Sardano (2000), McMullen and Strong (1997), Bowlin (1998), Basso and Funari (2001), and Morey and Morey (1999)).

Barr, Seiford, and Siems (1994), however, suggest that using a single input/output ratio to assess management quality is impractical, and propose using numerous variables (a multidimensional approach). Because the BCC model relaxed the convexity constraints enforced in the CCR model, it permits measurement of the efficiency of DMUs on a variable returns to scale. The convexity constraint guarantees the unit is of similar scale size as the unit being measured. The efficiency score obtained from the BCC model is at least equal to that obtained from the CCR model.

On the other hand, the CCR model is the first and primary DEA model based on efficiency. It allows a set of optimal weights to be calculated for each variable (input and output) to maximize a unit's efficiency score. If these weights are applied to any other unit in the data set, the efficiency score would not exceed 100. The CCR model's overall score aggregates both pure technical efficiency and scale efficiency. Despite the many modified DEA models in existence, the CCR model is still the most broadly known and used. Basically, the BCC and CCR models offer two ways of considering the same problem.

The notion of cross-evaluation was first seen in Sexton, Silkman, and Hogan (1986), and later in Oral, Ketani, and Lang (1991), Thanassoulis, Boussofiane, and Dyson (1995), and Doyle and Green (1994). As we note earlier, cross-evaluation is superior to either basic DEA method because 1) efficiency is still measured relative to the FOF with the highest efficiency score, but 2) having more than one combination of weights of a fund that maximizes its own efficiency adds an extra dimension of flexibility. The main idea of DEA is that it is flexible and can branch out to other FOFs to evaluate their individual performance. FOFs with high average efficiency from a cross-efficiency matrix are a good example for inefficient funds to work toward and improve their methods.

A cross-efficiency matrix consists of rows and columns (i x j), each equal to the number of units in the analysis. The efficiency of unit j is computed with the optimal weights for unit i. The higher the values in column j, the more likely that j is an efficient fund using good operating and guiding principles.

The super-efficiency method goes even further to identify and differentiate FOFs that have achieved a score of 100 in the basic model. Because these funds can achieve a higher score in the super-efficiency model, pension funds and other investors can obtain a further measure of comparison for the most efficient FOFs.

Strengths of DEA

DEA can manage multiple input and output models and it does not presuppose that inputs and outputs are dependent or related. DEA uses individual data points, not averages. Charnes and Cooper (1985) emphasize that DEA can measure inefficient units and feature areas of improvement for each one, as well as a best method or optimal frontier rather than just traditional averages.

Limitations of DEA

The characteristics that make DEA so powerful can also be problematic, however. DEA assumes that the inputs and outputs have no errors. Also, an appropriate number of funds must be considered in the analysis to have a proper working sample. But the main drawback of DEA may be that it can interpret how well a FOF is doing compared to its peers, but it cannot compare it to a theoretical maximum. As Miller and Noulas (1996) note, determining whether hedge funds are inefficient relative to others does not primarily result in a maximum output for a given level of input.

DATA AND METHODOLOGY

We adopt and expand the methodology of Sedzro and Sardano (2000), who investigated mutual funds, and apply it to hedge fund classifications using the basic, cross-efficiency, and super-efficiency models. Of course, since FOFs exhibit non-normal distributions and non-linear returns, we must use different variables than those used for mutual funds.

The inputs and outputs must correspond to the activities of the FOFs in order for the analysis to make sense. We use six variables in a risk-return framework, three for inputs and three for outputs, since a larger number might clutter the interpretation. Modern portfolio theory measures the total risk of a portfolio by using the variance of the returns. But this method does not separate the upside risk, which investors seek, from the downside returns they want to avoid. Variance is not typically a good method for measuring risk, but semi-variance is frequently used and accepted in the investment area. Semi-variance does measure the downside risk. The skewness for a normal symmetrical distribution will in effect be close to zero. Negative skewness implies that the data are skewed to the left; positive skewness implies the data are skewed to the right. Returns above the mean can hardly be regarded as risky by investors, but the variance below the mean provides more information during extreme market events which confirms that investors worry more about underperformance than overperformance (Markowitz (1991)). Extreme market events include the following: the Tequila crisis of 1994, the Asian currency crisis of 1997, the Russian ruble crisis of 1998, and the September 11, 2001 terrorist attacks.

The inputs are: 1) lower mean monthly semi-skewness, 2) lower mean monthly semi-variance, and 3) mean monthly lower return. The outputs are: 1) upper mean semi-skewness, 2) upper mean semi-variance, and 3) mean monthly upper return. The risk-free rate used is the ninety-day monthly U.S. T-bill rate.

We evaluate the performance of FOFs and determine whether they are efficient. The value of outputs is the value-added of each FOF. We received the Zurich Capital Markets (ZCM) hedge fund data from LaPorte Asset Allocation System and examine the efficiency of the FOF classification for the 1997-2001 and 1999-2001 periods using the same 182 FOFs (we believe that a seven- or ten-year examination period would have resulted in significantly fewer funds). The data were aggregated into separate DEA runs for the three-year and five-year periods. This enables us to see whether the rankings differ during both periods. Our data set consists of monthly returns net of all management and performance fees. We do not examine defunct FOFs.

EMPIRICAL RESULTS

Tables 4.1 and 4.2 show DEA results for the FOFs that achieved an efficiency score of 100 for the 1997-2001 and 1999-2001 periods. We do not show FOFs that received less than 100. The basic DEA score is then compared with the efficiency scores achieved using the cross- and super-efficiency models. An efficiency score of 100 signifies that a FOF is efficient and that no other fund has produced better outputs with the inputs used. This does not imply that all funds with a score of 100 provide the same return during the examination period, however, just that the "return is at the maximum of the incurred risk." The efficiency score is not absolute. A FOF with an efficiency score of 100 returning 20 percent is considered more risky than a FOF with a score of 100 returning 15 percent. Note that the results obtained from DEA do not guarantee future efficiency, but it is nonetheless a very valuable selection and screening tool. Every FOF with an efficiency score of 100 can be considered as one of the best.

Basic efficiency is perhaps not quite enough to assess the performance appraisal of FOFs, though, because cross-efficiency and super-efficiency go beyond self-appraisal to peer appraisal (Vassiloglou and Giokas (1990),

Table 4.1
Comparison of Basic DEA 100% Efficient, Cross and Super Efficient Funds of Hedge Funds, 1997-2001

FUNDS OF HEDGE FUNDS	*5 Year Basic Efficiency Score DEA BCC Model*	*5 Year Cross Efficiency Score DEA BCC Model*	*5 Year Super Efficiency Score DEA BCC Model*
GAM TRADING	100	66.55	114.55
GAM TRADING FUND {EURO}	100	70.37	183.77
LAFAYETTE EUROPE FUND {EURO}	100	78.69	125.60
LEVERAGED GLOBAL	100	62.29	116.25
ONTARIO PARTNERS	100	60.39	145.26
PRIME ADVISORS FUND LTD.	100	90.88	131.09
SELECT CASH ENHANCEMENT	100	44.85	999.00
SANDALDEBT	100	64.61	497.55
WIMBLEDON FUND (C)	100	91.43	143.16

Table 4.2
Comparison of Basic DEA 100% Efficient, Cross and Super Efficient Funds of Hedge Funds, 1999-2001

FUNDS OF HEDGE FUNDS	*5 Year Basic Efficiency Score DEA BCC Model*	*5 Year Cross Efficiency Score DEA BCC Model*	*5 Year Super Efficiency Score DEA BCC Model*
AGGRESSIVE PRIME ADVISORS	100	27.03	263.58
AIG DKR INTL RELATIVE VALUE FUND	100	59.93	120.95
CSAM FOF G7 EQUITY LONG / SHORT	100	72.36	102.56
ENHANCED INCOME FUND	100	40.53	147.98
GAM TRADING FUND	100	65.78	110.89
GEMS RUSSIA FUND	100	51.41	500.63
GLL INVESTORS	100	57.42	110.84
IRONWOOD PARTNERS	100	62.23	106.83
LAFAYETTE EURO FUND {EURO}	100	84.95	192.80
LEVERAGED GLOBAL OPPORTUNITY FUND	100	44.02	160.11
LIGHTHOUSE SUPER CASH FUND	100	38.29	136.70
ONTARIO PARTNERS	100	69.25	999.00
PARADIGM EQUITIES	100	71.62	104.72
PEABODY GLOBAL PARTNERS	100	76.52	128.33
PREASIDIS	100	61.87	109.74
REMBRANDT (B)	100	65.24	164.89
SANDALDEBT	100	63.26	626.76
SELECT CASH ENHANCEMENT	100	47.25	999.00
WIMBLEDON FUND (C)	100	86.49	201.34

Sedzro and Sardano (2000)). FOFs with an efficiency score of 100 drop in value when the average cross-efficiency measure is used. It may be possible that one or a few hedge fund strategies within a FOF could dominate and may affect the performance for a particular year.

We identify the "champion" fund of hedge funds. The score implies the number of times an efficient fund has been part of an inefficient FOF's reference set as a result of basic DEA analysis. As the frequency of a FOF appearing in a reference set increases, the likelihood of the fund being a good performer increases. The efficient FOF appearing in the most reference sets can be considered the overall "champion," and can help inefficient funds learn from their superior management and investment practices. The Banxia software (www.banxia.com) was used for the basic and cross-efficiency models; the Warwick software was used for the super-efficiency model. The champion funds were calculated using the basic DEA model. The Banxia software generated Paradigm Equities as the overall champion for the 1999-2001 period, while the Lafayette Europe Fund over the same period had the highest cross-efficiency score. The 1997-2001 "champion" is the Prime Advisors Fund; the 1999-2001 "champion" is the Lafayette Europe Fund.

Cross-efficiency displays the scores that each FOF would achieve by using the optimal weights for each other FOF as generated by the DEA analysis. Large differences in the relative scores may indicate that they specialize in diverse things (the combination percentage of the hedge fund strategies within FOFs may be different). The higher the cross efficiency score implies the fund has achieved the highest average by its peers. In other words the fund has performed well in all areas. The Babe Ruth analogy is a classic example. Babe Ruth was a great home run hitter and in terms of simple efficiency (basic DEA model) he would have achieved a score of 100, but if he was to be compared to other players on the team, he may not have been an all around player thus making his cross efficiency score low compared to an all around good player.

We find that the Wimbledon Fund {C} during the 1997-2001 and 1999-2001 periods had the highest cross-efficiency score. During the same periods, Select Cash Enhancement achieved the highest super efficiency score. Many funds attaining a score of 100 in the basic DEA model may not have achieved super efficiency; however, these funds are still efficient.

Despite the often incomplete disclosure and transparency of hedge funds, our aim is to examine which FOFs are efficient. Once identified, one can further observe their techniques and learn on how to become more efficient. Do they use active or passive management? How many hedge funds do they have in their portfolio? What percentage do they allocate to various hedge fund strategies? And, finally, how do they perform manager selection? The answers to all these questions may illustrate why the most efficient fund is the best.

CONCLUSION

Data Envelopment Analysis can assist pension funds, institutional investors, and high-net worth individuals with choosing the most efficient funds of hedge funds. It can also be used as an alternative selection tool to assist FOF managers in picking hedge funds. We believe DEA is an excellent complement to other risk-adjusted measures and helps obtain a more complete picture of FOF performance.

Cross-efficiency, as discussed in Doyle and Green (1991, 1994), and super-efficiency, as discussed in Andersen and Petersen (1993), provide pension funds with even more powerful tools. Having a high cross-efficient or super-efficient FOF is highly desirable. As the DEA method slowly becomes accepted and used by more academics, money managers, and pension funds, its functional ability will improve the process of selecting efficient and good-performing funds.

Future research using other DEA models could examine managed futures and CTA classifications. It would also be interesting to measure the efficiency of various hedge fund indices from database vendors, such as Hedge Fund Research (HFR), EACM, ALTVEST, and TASS.

Appendix

We adapt the notation from Adler, Friedman, and Stern (2002) for the simple DEA, cross-efficiency, and super-efficiency models. By comparing n units with s outputs, denoted by y_{rk} in Equation (1), where $r = 1, \ldots,$ s, and m inputs denoted by x_{ik}, $i = 1, \ldots, m$, the efficiency measure for fund k is:

$$h_k = Max \frac{\sum_{r=1}^{s} u_r y_{rk}}{\sum_{i=1}^{m} v_i x_{ik}}, \tag{1}$$

where the weights u_r and v_i are positive. Another set of constraints requires that the same weights, when applied to all funds, do not provide any individual fund with an efficiency score greater than 100 percent. This condition is present in the following set of constraints:

$$\frac{\sum_{r=1}^{s} u_r y_{rj}}{\sum_{i=1}^{m} v_i x_{ij}} \leq 1 \quad \text{for } j = 1, \ldots, n$$

The efficiency score falls between 0 percent and 100 percent, with fund k regarded as efficient upon receiving an efficiency score of 100 percent. Therefore, each fund selects weights to maximize its own efficiency with respect to the constraints present (see Equation (2)).

$$h_k = Max \sum_{r=1}^{s} u_r y_{rk} + c_k$$

constraint:

$$\sum_{i=1}^{m} v_i x_{ij} - \sum_{r=1}^{s} u_r y_{rj} - c_{k \geq 0} \quad \text{for j=1,...n,} \tag{2}$$

$$\sum_{i=1}^{m} v_i x_{ik} = 1$$

$$u_r \geq 0 \quad \text{for } r = 1, \ldots, s,$$

$$v_i \geq 0 \quad \text{for } i = 1, \ldots, m.$$

An additional constant variable, denoted by c_k , is added in the BCC model to allow variable returns to scale. For a fund to be BCC technically efficient, its only requirement is to be efficient, but for a fund to be efficient in the CCR model, it must be both scale and technically efficient (Bowlin (1998)). A unit is scale efficient if the scale of its operation is optimal. If the scale is reduced or increased, the efficiency will weaken. A scale efficient unit functions at optimal returns to scale and can be calculated by dividing the total efficiency from the CCR model by the technical efficiency from the BCC model.

The equations show that the problem is generated n times in trying to distinguish the relative efficiency scores of all hedge funds. The cross-evaluation model we use here is represented by Equation (3):

$$h_{kj} = \frac{\sum_{r=1}^{s} u_{rk} y_{rj}}{\sum_{i=1}^{m} v_{ik} x_{ij}}, \; k = 1, \ldots, n, \; j = 1, \ldots, n. \qquad (3)$$

where h_{kj} is the score of fund j cross-evaluated by the weight of fund k. In the cross-evaluation matrix, all funds are bounded by $0 \leq h_{kj} \leq 1$, and the funds in the diagonal, h_{kk}, depict the simple DEA efficiency score, $h_{kk} = 1$ for efficient funds and $h_{kk} < 1$ for inefficient funds.

Super-efficiency eliminates the kth constraint in Equation (4).

$$h_k = Max \sum_{r=1}^{s} u_r y_{rk}$$

constraint:

$$\sum_{i=1}^{m} v_i x_{ij} - \sum_{r=1}^{s} u_r y_{rj} \geq 0 \text{ for } j = 1, \ldots, n, j \neq k, \qquad (4)$$

$$\sum_{i=1}^{m} v_i x_{ij} = 1,$$

$$u_r \geq \varepsilon \text{ for } r = 1, \ldots, s,$$

$$v_i \geq \varepsilon \text{ for } i = 1, \ldots, m.$$

CHAPTER 5

Performance of the Ten Largest CTAs in Extreme Market Events and Negative S&P 500 Months

INTRODUCTION

Over the last decade, hedge funds have been the ideal choice for providing downside equity risk management for traditional stock and bond portfolios (Schneeweis, Spurgin, and McCarthy (1996); Schneeweis, Spurgin, and Potter (1996)). Research into the performance persistence of CTAs is sparse, so there is little information on the success of these managers over the last several years (Edwards and Ma (1988); Irwin, Krukemyer, and Zulauf (1992); Irwin, Zulauf, and Ward (1994); Kazemi (1996)). However, it is generally agreed that during bear markets, CTAs provide greater downside protection than hedge funds and have higher returns along with an inverse correlation to stock returns in bear markets (Edwards and Caglayan (2001b)). The benefits of CTAs are similar to those of hedge funds, in that they improve and may offer a superior risk adjusted return trade-off to stock and bond indices, and can act as diversifiers in investment portfolios (Schneeweis, Savanayana and McCarthy (1991)).

As of September 30, 2002, the ten largest CTAs in the Barclays CTA (BAR) database managed approximately $US 11.5 billion. What makes these mammoth-sized funds so successful? During the 1990-1998 period, the correlation of managed futures to the S&P 500 during its best 30 months was 0.33; during its worse 30 months it was -0.25. These results cannot easily be replicated through other investment alternatives. According to Schneeweis, Spurgin and Georgiev (2001), CTAs are known to short stock markets regularly. One disadvantage, however, is that during bull markets, their performance is usually less favorable than hedge funds (Georgiev (2001)).

Investors who include CTAs in their portfolios typically allocate only a small portion of their assets to these investment vehicles (Georgiev (2001)). Many investors are not aware that during increased periods of stock market volatility, careful inclusion of CTA managers into investment portfolios can improve a portfolio's return characteristics, especially during harsh bear markets (Schneeweis, Spurgin, and Georgiev (2001); Schneeweis and Georgiev (2002)). Notably, throughout international financial markets during this past decade, periods of extreme volatility did not really affect CTAs. In fact, it was during these periods of high volatility that CTAs made their money and produced superior returns.

DATA

We used the Barclay CTA (BAR) database for our study, which covered the period from January 1994 to September 2002. This time frame was selected because 1994 was a bad year for stock markets. In the following year, the heated bull market began and we wanted to see the impact it had on the ten largest CTAs. We therefore felt that this starting point made our study more pragmatic.

Our study encompasses major extreme market events such as the Asian currency crisis of October 1997, the Russian ruble crisis of August 1998, and the events of September 11, 2001, along with the largest monthly drops in the S&P 500 Index during the examination period. The five classifications of CTAs in the BAR database are Financials, Currency, Diversified, Energy, and Agricultural. However, there is a small group of CTAs that have an unassigned subtype in the database. The returns used are net of all management and performance fees, and our data only examine live funds. The LaPorte Asset Allocation System Software is used to generate statistics.

The performance returns and various descriptive statistics of the top ten funds are displayed in Table 5.1 for the period January 1994 to September 2002. The funds are listed highest to lowest in terms of assets under management. We include the fund's Sharpe ratio (assuming a risk free rate of 4.25 percent), compounded return, standard deviation, along with various indicators of drawdown. The performance of the top funds during extreme market events are displayed in Table 5.2. The alphas and betas of each fund of hedge funds against the MSCI World Index, the S&P 500 Index, and the Salomon Aggregate Bond Index, are displayed in Table 5.3.

RESULTS

As indicated in Table 5.1, the majority of funds performed well during the period under consideration. Five funds achieved compounded returns of over 200 percent, but only one of them had Sharpe ratios greater than unity; this means high returns were also accompanied by high volatility in most of these funds. The five largest CTAs were not the top performers in the group (except for Grossman Asset Management) and did not have the highest Sharpe ratios. It is reassuring that a majority of these same funds did not need many periods to recover from their maximum drawdown (Table 5.1).

Only a handful of funds had alphas greater than one with the MSCI World and the S&P 500 indices (Table 5.2). However, most had alphas less than one with the Salomon Aggregate Bond Index. Most of the betas with the MSCI World and S&P 500 indices were negative, while most of them with the Salomon Aggregate Bond Index were positive; most of the betas are less than one. Table 5.2 also indicates that a great majority of the funds have a negative correlation with both the MSCI World and S&P 500 indices, but a positive correlation with the Salomon Aggregate Bond Index.

CONCLUSION

This study suggests that there are marked differences among the ten largest CTAs in terms of risk/return characteristics. Indeed, during our investigation period, many CTAs had low Sharpe ratios, low or negative correlations with the S&P 500 and the MSCI World index, and modest compounded returns, while others fared better. Many of these large CTAs are among the oldest in existence.

Although a recent report suggests that the survival time of CTAs is 24 months (Brown, Goetzmann, and Park (2001)), the CTAs in this study have lasted for much longer. Consequently, their survival rates are higher than usually reported in the literature. While their performance may not be outstanding, their longevity and ability to weather economic turmoil over the years cannot be denied. This suggests that pension funds can expect a trade-off between longevity and performance in large CTAs.

Table 5.1
Performance of the Largest CTAs January 1994-September 2002

Name	*Subtype*	*Ending Millions*	*Compounded Return*	*Sharpe Ratio*	*Annualized Standard Deviation*	*Maximum Drawdown*	*Periods in Maximum Drawdown*	*Periods to Recover from Maximum*	*Probability of Peak Capital Loss Drawdown*
Campbell & Co.	Financial	3,050	190.5	0.59	15.36	20.52	13	12	0.52
Bridgewater Associates Inc.	Financial	2,500	101.4	0.39	10.41	14.18	4	19	0.46
Grossman Asset Management	Currency	1,049	201.29	0.67	13.76	16.77	18	0	0.43
Crabel Capital Management	Unassigned	1,000	113.49	0.78	6.15	4.24	8	1	0.05
Chesapeake Capital Corp.	Diversified	848	116.18	0.32	15.52	19.17	13	0	0.64
Grunham Managed Funds Ltd.	Diversified	740	279.37	0.87	13.98	13.31	2	1	0.31
Rotella Capital Management Inc.	Diversified	640	341.43	1.16	12.33	11.86	4	13	0.16
Sunrise Capital Partners	Diversified	635	210.93	0.61	15.84	14.74	2	3	0.47
DUNN Capital Management	Financials	627	795.63	0.66	36.56	44.16	12	3	0.65
F/X Concepts Inc.	Currency	555	95.25	0.21	17.40	21.01	13	7	0.70

Table 5.2

Performance of the Largest CTAs in Extreme Events and the Worst Negative S&P 500 Months

Name	*October 1997*	*August 1998*	*Nov 2000*	*Feb 2001*	*Sept 2001*	*June 2002*	*July 2002*	*Sept 2002*
Campbell & Co.	2.39	9.23	5.98	0.71	6.94	7.74	7.64	4.1
Bridgewater Associates Inc.	−2.38	0.47	2.45	−2.39	−3.04	4.33	−3.40	−2.57
Grossman Asset Management	6.25	1.76	0.92	3.16	−9.00	−3.45	−4.97	−3.34
Crabel Capital Management	0.60	−2.00	−1.70	−0.47	−2.19	2.43	3.73	0.54
Chesapeake Capital Corp.	−2.34	7.27	7.42	3.75	7.15	4.23	2.81	3.85
Grunham Managed Funds Ltd.	0.35	9.48	5.52	1.42	5.50	7.87	2.79	3.20
Rotella Capital Management Inc.	−0.06	16.5	6.81	1.67	7.22	6.59	4.68	3.82
Sunrise Capital Partners	−1.18	9.54	6.16	3.74	7.36	8.59	1.59	6.20
DUNN Capital Management	−0.60	27.5	28.00	0.55	1.13	24.24	14.82	9.11
F/X Concepts Inc.	0.58	−5.22	2.97	−3.25	−2.42	5.45	0.09	−0.14

Table 5.3
Alpha, Beta and Correlation of the Ten Largest CTAs with MSCI World, S&P 500 and the Salomon Bond Index, January 1994 to September 2002

	Relation with MSCI World Index			*Relation with S&P 500 Index*			*Relation with Salomon Aggregate Bond Index*		
CTA	*Alpha*	*Beta*	*Correlation*	*Alpha*	*Beta*	*Correlation*	*Alpha*	*Beta*	*Correlation*
Campbell & Co.	1.21	–0.15	–0.15	1.25	–0.13	–0.13	0.40	1.23	0.35
Bridgewater Associates Inc.	0.63	0.19	0.26	0.60	0.14	0.22	0.61	0.16	0.07
Grossman Asset Management	1.20	–0.15	–0.16	1.20	–0.08	–0.10	1.49	–0.58	–0.19
Crabel Capital Management	0.73	0.02	0.04	0.71	0.04	0.10	0.64	0.17	0.12
Chesapeake Capital Corp.	0.83	0.02	0.02	0.85	–0.01	–0.01	0.22	1.02	0.29
Grunham Managed Funds Ltd.	1.44	–0.20	–0.21	1.50	–0.18	–0.20	1.25	0.17	0.05
Rotella Capital Management Inc.	1.57	–0.20	–0.24	1.64	–0.20	–0.26	0.97	0.85	0.30
Sunrise Capital Partners	1.28	–0.21	–0.20	1.38	–0.24	–0.24	0.80	0.65	0.18
DUNN Capital Management	2.82	–0.42	–0.17	2.91	–0.34	–0.15	0.88	2.93	0.35
F/X Concepts Inc.	0.70	0.14	0.12	0.64	0.15	0.14	0.59	0.28	0.07

CHAPTER 6

Selecting Funds of Hedge Funds: A Survey of the Twenty Largest Funds

INTRODUCTION

Many pension funds have been adding more of their employees' hard earned money into funds of hedge funds (a basket of hedge funds) for downside equity risk management. As of July 2002, the twenty largest funds of hedge funds in the Zurich Capital Markets (ZCM) database managed approximately $US 10.4 billion. What makes these mammoth-sized funds of funds so successful is not only a proven track record, but also regular monitoring of their managers and due diligence.

In the ZCM database, we found nearly one half dozen defunct funds of hedge funds with assets greater than $500 million. These funds have not ceased operations; they have merely stopped reporting to database vendors, probably because their managers no longer wish to attract additional capital (Gregoriou (2002)). Investors need to consider not only the size of a fund of funds (in terms of assets), but also how many managers comprise it. Most of the top twenty funds of hedge funds in this study include roughly 20-25 hedge funds, which seems to be the ideal number for diversification (Gregoriou and Rouah (2002); Peskin et al. (2000)). While adding more funds can offer some benefits (such as very low volatility), additional funds can hamper the maneuverability of the fund of funds manager. Arguably, this would defeat the purpose of investing in a fund of funds. While a large fund of funds can absorb the administrative costs of monitoring an undue number of managers, such a strategy would require convincing evidence.

When constructing a fund of hedge funds, any potential hedge fund manager must be completely transparent because hedge funds are not bound by Investment Company Act (1941) regulations on disclosure. If a hedge fund manager is not willing to provide performance numbers regularly, does not provide annual reports that describe the objectives and goals of the fund, or restricts any other information on the fund or on its personnel, stay away! It is only through active management of a fund of hedge funds that timely entry and exit of managers can be determined. Keeping the same managers over many years in a passive strategy may result in its premature demise.

All funds of funds in this study actively oversee the operations of their hedge fund managers in order to monitor the fund and its activities, such as changes in personnel or investment style. Well managed funds conduct standardized person-to-person interviews with each manager at least once per month to discuss the manager's economic outlook and its impact on the sectors within which the fund is operating. Some fund of hedge funds managers assign a points system to each fund, based on characteristics such as transparency, track record, and future performance objectives. Industry professionals have often pointed out that managing a fund of funds is a "people business" more than a "money business." Certainly Rothschild's Leveraged Capital Holdings (the oldest fund of hedge funds) would agree, as it has been interviewing its managers regularly since the fund was started in 1969.

DATA

The data for our study consists of monthly returns net of all fees ranked in terms of assets under management as of July 31, 2002. The 91 monthly returns of funds of hedge funds from January 1995 to July 2002 were obtained from the ZCM Hedge Fund database, which includes both offshore and onshore funds. The LaPorte Asset Allocation System Software is used to generate statistics. This time frame was selected because 1995 was the year the feverish bull market began and we wanted to see the impact it had on the twenty largest funds of hedge funds. We therefore felt that this starting point made our study more pragmatic.

The performance returns and various descriptive statistics of the top twenty funds of hedge funds are displayed in Table 1 for the period

January 1995 to July 2002. The funds are listed highest to lowest in terms of assets under management. We include the fund's Sharpe ratio (assuming a risk free rate of 4.25 percent), compounded return, standard deviation, along with various indicators of drawdown. The alphas and betas of each fund of funds against the MSCI World Index, the S&P 500 Index, and the Salomon Aggregate Bond Index, are displayed in Table 2.

RESULTS

As indicated in Table 6.1, the majority of funds performed well during the period under consideration. Six funds achieved compounded returns of over 200 percent, but only two of them had Sharpe ratios greater than unity, meaning high returns are also accompanied by high volatility in most of these funds. The largest five funds of hedge funds were not the top performers in the group and did not have the highest Sharpe ratios. It is reassuring that these same funds did not need many periods to recover from their maximum drawdown (Table 6.1).

Only a handful of funds had alphas greater than one with the MSCI World and the S&P 500 indices (Table 6.2). However, most had alphas greater than one with the Salomon Aggregate Bond Index. Most of the betas with the MSCI World and S&P 500 indices were positive, while most of them with the Salomon Aggregate Bond Index were negative, and all betas were less than one. Table 6.2 also indicates that almost one half of the funds have a high correlation (greater than 0.5) with both the MSCI World and S&P 500 indices. Hausmann Holdings (the largest funds of hedge funds in this study) was found to have the highest correlation with both of these indices.

CONCLUSION

This study suggests that there are marked differences among the twenty largest funds of hedge funds in terms of risk-return characteristics. Indeed, during our investigation period, many funds of funds had low Sharpe ratios, high correlations with market indices, and modest compounded returns, while others fared better. Many of these large funds of funds are among the oldest in existence.

Table 6.1.
Performance of the Twenty Largest Funds of Hedge Funds
January 1995 to July 2002

Funds of Hedge Funds	*Millions Ending July 31, 2002*	*Compounded Return*	*Annualized Standard Deviation*	*Annualized Sharpe Ratio*	*Probability Next Year's Return is Above 7%*	*Maximum Drawdown (Peak to Valley)*	*Periods to Recover from Maximum Drawdown*	*Highest Period Return*	*Lowest Period Return*
Hausmann Holdings	2,500	127.78	11.07	0.66	.64	16.99	0	9.50	−9.00
Permal Investment Holdings	1,500	122.49	12.31	0.58	.62	17.80	0	10.15	−13.59
GAM Diversity Fund	1,357	195.38	9.37	1.13	.78	11.91	6	10.13	−7.92
Olympia Star Series	1,085	146.77	6.45	1.23	.79	3.94	4	6.82	−2.73
Leveraged Capital Holdings	800	146.41	12.76	0.67	.65	22.41	0	13.03	−11.45
GAM Trading Fund	455	229.51	5.65	2.08	.94	1.91	2	7.24	−1.91
Asian Capital Holdings Fund	330	22.64	15.11	-1.00	.39	37.32	12	14.02	−9.71
GAM Multi Europe Fund	304	205.95	13.06	0.87	.72	19.39	13	15.98	−14.16
Prima Capital Fund	303	94.31	9.86	0.51	.58	19.27	0	7.52	−12.02
GAM Multi-Europe Fund (EURO)	253	243.20	15.70	0.85	.72	19.44	10	16.95	−13.88
La Fayette Holdings	221	226.20	13.70	0.90	.74	19.92	12	18.10	−11.71
Greenway Investments (EURO)	212	70.50	4.67	0.62	.53	12.69	14	4.18	−6.78
Global Hedge Fund (SWF)	162	65.22	4.08	0.61	.49	9.98	8	3.83	−5.62
Sperry Complete Manager Fund	145	123.26	10.87	0.64	.64	12.42	5	10.57	−9.25
GAM Emerging Markets	138	41.33	18.48	0.11	.45	42.85	11	18.13	−14.05
CSAM G7 Equity Long Short Fund	137	278.36	8.26	1.67	.90	8.02	5	9.71	−7.95
GAM Trading Fund	134	218.33	11.88	0.99	.76	12.20	2	16.77	−12.20
GEMS Low Volatility Fund	123	107.27	3.13	1.74	.82	3.44	3	3.97	−1.47
Permal Emerging Markets	119	56.92	14.69	0.19	.48	39.62	0	10.54	−14.80
Wafra Starvest Funds	118	94.10	11.18	0.46	.57	18.78	14	8.02	−11.51

Table 6.2
Alpha, Beta, and Correlation of Twenty Largest Hedge Funds with MSCI World, S&P 500 and Salomon Bond Index, January 1995 to July 2002

	Relation with MSCI World Index			*Relation with S&P 500 Index*			*Relation with Salomon Aggregate Bond Index*		
Funds of Hedge Funds	*Alpha*	*Beta*	*Correlation*	*Alpha*	*Beta*	*Correlation*	*Alpha*	*Beta*	*Correlation*
Hausmann Holdings	0.69	0.49	0.65	0.53	0.43	0.63	0.95	0.02	0.01
Permal Investment Holdings	0.68	0.47	0.56	0.55	0.40	0.52	1.01	−0.09	−0.03
GAM Diversity Fund	1.07	0.29	0.46	1.01	0.23	0.39	1.35	−0.17	−0.08
Olympia Star Series	0.98	0.05	0.12	0.97	0.05	0.12	0.67	0.51	0.33
Leveraged Capital Holdings	0.70	0.65	0.74	0.48	0.58	0.74	1.15	−0.13	−0.04
GAM Trading Fund	1.34	−0.01	−0.03	1.35	−0.02	−0.06	1.15	0.27	0.20
Asian Capital Holdings Fund	0.04	0.49	0.48	−0.04	0.35	0.38	0.81	−0.73	−0.20
GAM Multi Europe Fund	1.03	0.49	0.56	0.91	0.39	0.49	1.61	−0.45	−0.15
Prima Capital Fund	0.49	0.51	0.76	0.31	0.46	0.76	0.86	0.13	−0.05
GAM Multi-Europe Fund (EURO)	1.17	0.53	0.50	1.03	0.43	0.45	2.13	−0.98	−0.27
La Fayette Holdings	1.19	0.35	0.38	1.13	0.25	0.29	1.37	0.02	0.01
Greenway Investments (EURO)	0.54	0.10	0.33	0.52	0.08	0.28	0.62	−0.03	−0.03
Global Hedge Fund (SWF)	0.51	0.09	0.31	0.49	0.07	0.28	0.68	−0.18	−0.19
Sperry Complete Manager Fund	0.71	0.41	0.55	0.60	0.33	0.49	1.13	−0.29	−0.11
GAM Emerging Markets	0.20	0.58	0.46	0.11	0.41	0.36	1.37	−1.26	−0.29
CSAM G7 Equity Long Short Fund	1.32	0.33	0.58	1.20	0.29	0.58	1.62	−0.18	−0.09
GAM Trading Fund	1.28	0.10	0.13	1.22	0.11	0.16	1.31	0.04	0.01
GEMS Low Volatility Fund	0.78	0.06	0.27	0.76	0.05	0.25	0.88	−0.11	−0.15
Permal Emerging Markets	0.29	0.53	0.53	0.13	0.45	0.50	1.05	−0.68	−0.20
Wafra Starvest Funds	0.50	0.51	0.68	0.35	0.43	0.63	0.98	−0.29	−0.11

A recent report found the 50 percent survival time of funds of hedge funds to be 7.5 years (Gregoriou (2002)), the highest among the ten hedge fund classifications examined. The funds of funds in this study have lasted for much longer. Regular monitoring and due diligence has allowed them to adapt to changing market and economic conditions by timely turnover of hedge fund managers. Consequently, they have survived much longer than usually reported in the literature. While their performance may not be outstanding, their longevity and ability to weather economic turmoil over the years cannot be denied. This suggests that pension funds can expect a trade-off between longevity and performance in large funds of hedge funds.

SECTION 2

COINTEGRATION, RANDOM WALKS, AND NON-STATIONARITY

Summary

In this section we examine the stochastic properties of hedge funds, and of managed futures, another popular alternative investment. In Chapter 7 we use cointegration to investigate the long-term relationships between the ten largest hedge funds in the MAR/Laporte database, and four stock market indices, over a ten-year period. We find that most of the time series examined contain one unit root. Of the hedge funds examined, Zweig-DiMenna International is cointegrated with the NASDAQ, while Perry Partners is cointegrated with the Morgan Stanley Capital International World Index (MSCI). The remaining hedge funds are not cointegrated with any of the other stock market indices under consideration. The study presented in this chapter suggests that large hedge funds do not track stock market indices.

Chapter 8 examines whether the Net Asset Value (NAV) of managed futures follow random walks. Monthly data from January 1990 to December 2000 are tested for nonstationarity and random walk with drift, using the Augmented Dickey-Fuller test. All of the managed futures classifications are nonstationary, but on the other hand, none are found to behave as random walks. Even when random walk behavior is allowed, evidence of positive drift parameters ensures that the NAVs contain discernable trends. We conclude that historical NAVs can be used to create reliable predictive models of managed futures.

Finally, Chapter 9 investigates whether hedge fund returns follow random walks. Monthly median returns data from January 1991 to December 2000, are tested for nonstationarity and random walk with drift, using the Augmented Dickey-Fuller test. All hedge fund classes except Market Neutral are found to be random walks, and most classes show evidence of a significant positive drift parameter. The stable returns and low volatility associated with the non-directional nature of the Market Neutral class could partly explain why time series of their returns contain discernable trends, rather than exhibiting random walk behavior. The conclusion of this Section, that hedge fund investment represents a viable long-term strategy, should be welcomed by derivative specialists and hedge fund managers.

CHAPTER 7

Do Stock Market Indices Move The Ten Largest Hedge Funds? A Cointegration Approach

INTRODUCTION

Hedge funds are becoming mainstream investments and their performance has been the subject of recent research, often with mixed results (Ackermann, *et al.* (1999); Agarwal and Naik (2000b)). While many studies have noted that hedge funds tend to outperform market indices during bear markets and underperform during bull markets (Edwards and Caglayan (2001b)), none have attempted to find long-term relationships between the two. Do large hedge funds and market indices move together?

Several authors have concluded that hedge funds are powerful diversification tools, either for inclusion in traditional stock, bond, and currency portfolios, or as stand-alone investments. At the same time, they reduce risk and increase risk-adjusted returns (Sharpe ratio) of portfolios (Schneeweis and Spurgin (1998a)). Furthermore, hedge funds provide a better risk-return tradeoff than mutual funds (Liang (1999); Diz (2000)).

Cointegration has previously been applied in analyses of stock market indices (Kasa (1992); Ghosh, Saidi, and Johnson (1999)). However, the purpose of this chapter is to examine whether there exist common long-term trends between the ten largest hedge funds when compared to the S&P 500 Index, the Morgan Stanley Capital International World Index (MSCI), Russell 2000, and the NASDAQ, over a ten-year period. Although most hedge funds and market indices are non-stationary time series, the presence of cointegrating relationships would imply that useful forecasting models could be envisaged. It stands to reason that, by being aware of the synchronicity between hedge funds and market indices, investors could better time the entry and exit of hedge fund holdings in their portfolios.

DATA AND METHODOLOGY

The database consists of 1,484 offshore and onshore live hedge funds that report results to LaPorte Asset Allocation System/Managed Account Reports (MAR/Laporte). We use 120 monthly observations spanning the period from January 1991 to December 2000. In our analyses, we use the net asset value (NAV) and the closing monthly value for each hedge fund and market index, respectively.

The MAR database calculates the net asset value using net of all fees, and separates a total of 1,484 live offshore and onshore funds into the following ten classes: Event Driven, Global International, Global Established, Global Emerging, Global Macro, Market Neutral, Fund of Hedge Funds, Short Sellers, Long Only, and Sector. For our purposes, we only examine the ten largest hedge funds with the starting point of January 1991 and ending in December 2000, defined in terms of total capital under management as of December 2000. These are presented in Table 7.1. Our study suffers from several limitations. Survivorship bias is inherent in

Table 7.1
Investment Style and Capital Under Management January 1991-December 2000, for the Ten Largest Hedge Funds in MAR/Laporte

Name of Hedge Fund	*Style*	*Capital at Dec 2000 ($ million)*
Caxton / Gam Fund	Global International	728
Cypress Partners	Global Macro	939
Kingdon Offshore (A)	Global Established	2,483
Maverick Fund	Global Established	4,300
Millenium International	Market Neutral	812
Orbis Optimal	Global International	735
Perry Partners	Event Driven	1,663
Quantum Endowment Fund	Global Macro	2,554
Tiger	Global Macro	2,000
Zweig-DiMenna International	Global Established	2,763

Source: www.marhedge.com

the MAR/Laporte database, but since we are examining the ten largest hedge funds only, this is not likely to be a problem. More importantly, our analyses are hampered by the use of monthly data, which are known to provide inferior estimates than daily data. Unfortunately, hedge fund database vendors provide monthly data only.

We did not use the logs of the time series in our analyses, but this is a choice rather than a weakness. While logs will stabilize variances that increase with the level of the series (one form of heteroscedasticity), they do render interpretation of parameter estimates more difficult. Lastly, selection bias could be a problem, since growing hedge funds are liable to stop reporting their results to database vendors out of fear that size could eventually have a negative impact on their future performance.

Non-stationarity, unit root tests, and cointegration are subjects that are thoroughly dealt with in many textbooks on time-series and econometrics (Hamilton (1994); Gujarati (1995); Pindyck and Rubinfeld (1998)). To test for cointegration among two or more non-stationary time series, it must first be determined that each series contains only one unit root – this implies that only first-order differencing will be required to render them stationary. The Augmented Dickey-Fuller test (ADF) has become one of the most popular unit root tests in econometrics. In its most general form, including intercept and trend, it specifies the following regression model for the monthly observation, Y_t

$$Y_t - Y_{t-1} = \alpha + \beta t + (\rho - 1)Y_{t-1} + \sum_{i=1}^{p} \lambda_i \Delta Y_{t-i} + \varepsilon_t \, , \tag{1}$$

where p, the number of lags, must be chosen large enough so that the residuals ε_t are white noise. A t-statistic (called the tau statistic) is computed to test for the presence of a unit root (i.e., to test whether the regression parameter $\rho - 1 = 0$, or equivalently, whether $\rho = 1$). Since the t-statistic does not follow a t-distribution, its values must be compared to critical values obtained by Dickey and Fuller, which were subsequently updated (Davidson and McKinnon (1993)).

One drawback of the ADF test is that it loses power for high values of p. Another option is to employ the Phillips-Perron test (PP), which specifies the following characterization

$$Y_t = a_0 + b_1 Y_{t-1} + u_t \, , \tag{2}$$

where the u_t's are serially correlated and possible heteroscedastic.

After it is established by the ADF and PP tests, that each hedge fund and market index series contains one unit root, the "two-stage" estimation procedure is applied. In the first stage, a regression is run on the following cointegration equation with intercept

$$HF_t = a + bMI_t + e_t \, , \tag{3}$$

where HF_t represents the hedge fund, MI_t the market index, and t the time component, and a and b are regression parameters. If the two time series are cointegrated, then the residuals $e_t = HF_t - a - bMI_t$ will be stationary. This is determined by an application of the ADF and PP tests: replace Y_t and its lagged values by e_t and its lagged values in equations (1) and (2), and repeat the analyses. We examine the Durbin-Watson (DW) statistic from equation (2); values significantly larger than zero are also an indication that the residuals are stationary.

In the second stage, estimates of e_t are used to construct a vector Error Correction Model (ECM). This model ensures that short-run deviations from the long-term equilibrium between HF_t and MI_t will be corrected. The ECM to be estimated in our case is:

$$\begin{aligned} \Delta HF_t &= \alpha_t + \gamma_t e_{t-1} + \sum_{i=1}^{m} \beta_{1i} \Delta HF_{t-i} + \sum_{i=1}^{m} \beta_{2i} \Delta MI_{t=i} + \varepsilon_{1t} \\ \Delta MI_t &= \alpha_2 + \gamma_2 e_{t-1} + \sum_{i=1}^{m} \beta_{3i} \Delta HF_{t-i} + \sum_{i=1}^{m} \beta_{4i} \Delta MI_{t=i} + \varepsilon_{2t} \end{aligned} \tag{4}$$

where m is large enough so that the residuals ε_{1t} and ε_{2t} are totally random (white noise). The number of lag lengths, m, is selected by examination of the Akaike (AIC) and Schwarz information criteria, along with the adjusted R^2.

EMPIRICAL RESULTS

The results of the augmented Dickey-Fuller and Phillips-Perron unit root tests, on each hedge fund and market index, are presented in Table 7.2. The ADF and PP tests on the original series indicate that all series except the Quantum Endowment Fund and Russell 2000 index are non-stationary (columns 2 and 3). For these two series, the ADF and PP test statistics are large enough (in absolute value) to reject the hypothesis of a unit root. In the remaining series, only first differences are required to achieve stationarity, indicating the presence of one unit root. Evidence in support of a single unit root is quite strong; indeed significance at 1 percent is achieved for most series (columns 4 and 5).

Table 7.2
Augmented Dickey-Fuller (ADF) and Phillips-Perron (PP) Tests of Unit Roots, for Ten Largest Hedge Funds and Selected Market Indices, on Original Series and First Differences

	Tests on Original Series		*Tests on First Differences*	
Hedge Fund	*ADF*	*PP*	*ADF*	*PP*
Caxton / Gam Fund	1.40	1.54	– 3.84**	–11.65***
Cypress Partners	1.52	1.68	– 4.96***	– 12.23***
Kingdon Offshore (A)	– 0.52	– 0.71	– 5.19***	– 9.14***
Maverick Fund	1.38	1.31	– 5.04***	–11.36***
Millenium International	2.03	2.50	– 3.90**	– 6.10***
Orbis Optimal	– 2.80	– 2.40	– 4.79***	– 7.83***
Perry Partners	– 0.58	– 0.94	– 5.90***	– 6.86***
Quantum Endowment Fund	– 3.47**	– 4.13***	– 5.73***	– 11.33***
Tiger	– 1.87	– 1.69	– 3.78**	– 7.44***
Zweig-DiMenna International	– 1.03	– 1.71	– 7.70***	– 11.03***
MSCI	–2.36	– 2.39	– 5.29***	– 12.35***
NASDAQ	–2.23	– 2.26	– 5.29***	– 10.17***
Russell 2000	–3.34**	– 3.97**	– 7.78***	– 10.84***
S&P500	–1.86	–1.84	– 4.92***	– 12.91***

*Denotes significance at the 10% level, ** at the 5% level, and *** at the 1% level

The outcomes of the cointegration tests are shown in Table 7.3. We found cointegrating relationships in only 2 of the 27 possible combinations (9 funds × 3 indices). Indeed, the Likelihood Ratio (LR) is large enough to reject the hypothesis of no cointegration for Zweig-DiMenna and the NASDAQ, as well as for Perry Partners and the MSCI, at the 1 percent significance level. In both combinations, the ADF statistics are large enough (in absolute value) to reject the hypothesis of non-stationarity of the residuals e_t at the 5 percent level, but the PP statistic is large enough for the Perry/MSCI relation only. However, values of the DW are large enough to reject the non-stationarity hypothesis in both cointegrating equations.

Table 7.3
Results of Cointegration Analyses for Hedge Funds and Market Indices

		ADF, PP, and DW Tests, for Residuals e_t Estimated From Equation (3)			*Parameter Estimates from Cointegrating Equation (3)*		
Regressand	*Regressor*	*ADF*	*PP*	*DW*	*LR*	*a*	*b*
Zweig-DiMenna	NASDAQ	−2.30**	−0.15	0.372*	22.97***	−3455.81	−10.07
							(0.80)
							(−12.60)
Perry Partners	MSCI	−2.01**	−2.03**	0.323*	25.22***	1286.14	−7.50
						(843.33)	(2.89)
						(1.53)	(−2.60)

*Denotes significance at the 10% level, ** at the 5% level, and *** at the 1% level Standard errors and t-statistics in parentheses.

Results of the vector Error Correction Model (4) are presented in Table 7.4. For Zweig/NASDAQ two lags were sufficient, while for the Perry/MSCI, four lags were needed. In both ECMs, it is found that the estimated coefficients are such that $\gamma_1 < 0$ and $b\gamma_2 > 0$, where b is the parameter of the cointegrating equation (3). When the errors e_{t-1} are large and positive, these conditions reduce the spread between HF_t and MI_t, thereby "correcting" the errors and restoring equilibrium between HF_t and MI_t in the long-run (Alexander (1999)).

The short run impacts are determined by the lagged variables DZWEIG, DNASDAQ, DPERRY, and DMSCI, many of which attain significance, in terms of estimates – more than twice their standard errors (Table 7.4, last column). In particular, positive lagged values indicate persistence in the short-run. Many of the lagged values in the Zweig/NASDAQ ECM are positive, but most in the Perry/MSCI ECM are negative (third column).

SUMMARY AND CONCLUSION

We have attempted to identify cointegration relationships between the monthly NAVs of the ten largest hedge funds, and the closing values from various stock market indices. Using unit root tests, we find that all series contain a single unit root, with the exception of the Quantum Endowment Fund and the Russell 2000 Index. However, we found evidence of cointegration in only two hedge fund/market index combinations – Zweig/NASDAQ and Perry/MSCI.

Table 7.4
Parameter Estimates for the Estimated Vector Error Correction Model (4)

	ZWEIG-DiMENNA and NASDAQ			
Regressand	*Regressor*	*Estimated Coefficient*	*Standard Error*	*t-statistic*
DZweig-DiMenna	Constant	191.5910	181.9510	1.05
	e(*t*-1)	–0.1095	0.0893	–1.23
	D(ZWEIG(*t*-1))	0.4509	0.2132	2.12
	D(ZWEIG(*t*-2))	0.1506	0.2189	0.69
	D(NASDAQ(*t*-1))	–5.3163	2.2840	–2.33
	D(NASDAQ(*t*-2))	1.3949	2.0433	0.68
DNASDAQ	Constant	–8.6400	17.2507	–0.50
	e(*t*-1)	–0.0284	0.0085	–3.35
	D(ZWEIG(*t*-1))	0.0966	0.0202	4.78
	D(ZWEIG(*t*-2))	0.0444	0.0208	2.14
	D(NASDAQ(*t*-1))	–0.9067	0.2165	–4.19
	D(NASDAQ(*t*-2))	–0.1509	0.1937	–0.78

	PERRY PARTNERS and MSCI			
Regressand	*Regressor*	*Estimated Coefficient*	*Standard Error*	*t-statistic*
DPerry Partners	Constant	–	–	–
	e(*t*-1)	–0.0271	0.0056	–4.80
	D(PERRY(*t*-1))	0.3792	0.1087	3.49
	D(PERRY(*t*-2))	0.0509	0.1145	0.44
	D(PERRY(*t*-3))	0.0096	0.1154	0.08
	D(PERRY(*t*-4))	–0.1813	0.1042	–1.74
	D(MSCI(*t*-1))	–0.0001	0.2177	–0.01
	D(MSCI(*t*-2))	–0.3726	0.2314	–1.61
	D(MSCI(*t*-3))	–0.3278	0.2315	–1.42
	D(MSCI(*t*-4))	–0.3627	0.2263	–1.60
DMSCI	Constant	–	–	–
	e(*t*-1)	–0.0072	0.0029	–2.48
	D(PERRY(*t*-1))	0.0712	0.0558	1.28
	D(PERRY(*t*-2))	–0.0513	0.0588	–0.87
	D(PERRY(*t*-3))	–0.0219	0.0593	–0.37
	D(PERRY(*t*-4))	–0.0979	0.0535	–1.83
	D(MSCI(*t*-1))	–0.2617	0.1118	–2.34
	D(MSCI(*t*-2))	–0.1138	0.1189	–0.96
	D(MSCI(*t*-3))	0.0090	0.1189	0.08
	D(MSCI(*t*-4))	0.0096	0.1162	0.08

D(.) denotes the first difference operator and (*t*-i) the *i*th lag.

One possible explanation for the results is that Zweig-DiMenna, a Global Established fund that concentrates primarily on small or large cap U.S. stocks, uses a flexible long/short equity strategy, thus accounting for the co-movement in prices between Zweig-DiMenna and the NASDAQ Index during the investigation period. On the other hand, Perry Partners (an Event Driven fund) concentrates on merger arbitrage and takeover situations on a global level. Because of the increased activity in mergers and acquisitions in Europe during the last few years, Perry Partners has benefited from its non-U.S. exposure of this activity making it cointegrated with the MSCI.

The majority of hedge funds examined in this study were not cointegrated with any of the stock market indices under consideration. One possible explanation could be that the greatly magnified active trading strategies, along with the large amount of capital under management of large hedge funds, tend to be allocated over a wider variety of stock market indices, futures, options, currencies, swaps, and other derivative instruments.

CHAPTER 8

Nonstationarity Tests of Managed Futures

INTRODUCTION

This chapter investigates whether monthly net asset values (NAVs) of managed futures classifications follow random walks. Prior studies have investigated the stochastic behavior of financial time series, such as stock prices and market indices. Often, these studies show that these series are nonstationary; moreover, they sometimes follow random walks. Unit root tests, such as the Augmented Dickey-Fuller (ADF) test and Phillips-Perron (PP) test, have become the two most popular procedures for determining nonstationarity in financial time series.

Many authors have concluded that research on the performance persistence of commodity futures has yielded mixed results, which makes them difficult to evaluate in this regard (Brorsen and Irwin (1985, 1987); Murphy (1986); Irwin and Landa (1987); Irwin, Krukemeyer, and Zulauf (1992); Irwin, Zulauf, and Ward (1994); Elton, Gruber, and Rentzler (1987)). However, it is generally agreed that during bear markets, commodity futures provide greater downside protection than hedge funds and traditional asset classes (such as stocks and bonds), making them an attractive addition to investment portfolios. Although the correlations between commodity futures returns and stock and bond returns differ slightly on a year-to-year basis, the goal of managed futures is to have zero correlation (or even negative correlation) to stock and bond markets.

According to Schneeweis, Savanayana and McCarthy (1991), public commodity pools enhance portfolios by offering a risk-adjusted return tradeoff superior to that of stock and bond markets. The benefits offered by public commodity pool managers cannot be easily replicated through other investment alternatives. During bull markets, however, the returns of public commodity pools are not, in general, as high as those of hedge funds (Georgiev, (2001)). Unlike stocks and bonds, commodity futures have played a minor role in investors' asset allocation decisions, even though prior research suggests that direct investment in managed futures provides diversification benefits (Schneeweis, Spurgin, and Potter (1996), Georgiev (2001)).

Still, one must consider the possibility that managed futures NAVs follow random walks as opposed to some discernable trend. If the NAVs do indeed follow random walks, then temporary shocks would tend to persist rather than dissipate by reversion to the mean level. In the financial literature, time series that are "mean reverting" possess the statistical property known as "second-order stationary," "weak stationary," or simply "stationary." These series have a constant mean and variance, and autocorrelations that depend only on the time lag. Nonstationarity in time series can be ascertained by testing for the presence of a unit root, using so-called *unit root tests* such as the Augmented Dickey-Fuller (ADF) test. However, if a series is found to be nonstationary by the ADF test, it does not necessarily imply that it behaves like a random walk, since random walks are but one example of nonstationary time series.

This investigation into random walks is important, because no managed futures strategy that relies only on historical NAVs can be continuously profitable if markets are efficient and the random walk hypothesis holds true. In this case, managed futures NAVs would be entirely unrelated to historical performance (Pindyck and Rubinfeld (1998)). We found this to be the case in a recent study into the stochastic behavior hedge fund returns (Gregoriou, Rouah, and Sedzro (2001)).

DATA AND METHODOLOGY

The data consist of managed futures indices from the Zurich Futures/LaPorte Asset Allocation System database, covering monthly NAVs (expressed as net of all fees) from January 1990 to December 2000. One hundred and thirty-two monthly observations are used for each managed futures index. For consistency, we decided to use 1990 as a common starting point for all indices, since a few indices had starting points in the late

1970s and the remaining started in 1990. For purposes of this chapter, the monthly NAV of each managed futures index will be employed. The indices employed for each classification do not suffer from survivorship bias. Since its inception in 1979, the Zurich futures fund benchmark has not suffered from survivorship bias.

It is well documented in the mutual fund literature that daily data provide better estimates than monthly data, and help increase the power of tests (Kothari and Warner (2001)). Unfortunately, vendors of alternative investment databases provide monthly data only. The Zurich database separates managed futures into the following six classifications, or indices: Offshore, Public, Private, Guaranteed, Multi-Advisor, and Single Advisor. The number of funds (or pools) in each index, along with assets as of December 2000, is presented in Table 8.1.

Table 8.1
Description of Zurich Capital Markets Managed Futures Indices

Fund Type	*Number of Funds*	*Assets ($billion) as of December, 2000*
Offshore Funds	126	5.3
Public Funds	89	3.8
Private Funds	126	1.6
Guaranteed Funds	15	0.6
Multi-Advisor Funds	41	1.2
Single Advisor Funds	80	3.0

Source: www.marhedge.com

We use the Augmented Dickey-Fuller (ADF) and Phillips-Perron (PP) test to determine nonstationarity. These methods are described in the Appendix at the end of this chapter.

EMPIRICAL ANALYSIS

We used up to four lags in the six managed futures indices under consideration, but realized that one lag was sufficient for the ε_t to be serially independent. The results of the ADF tests (equation (2)) with $p=1$, on the original series and on their first differences, are presented in Table 8.2, along with values of the Durbin-Watson statistic.

Table 8.2
ADF Test Statistics of Nonstationarity and Durbin-Watson Statistics of Serial Correlation (Equation (2) with $p=1$), for Monthly Managed Futures Mean NAVs (1990-2000), on Original and First-Differenced Series

Managed Futures Trading Advisor Index	*ADF Statistic (DW Statistic)* Original series Y_t	First Differenced series W_t
Offshore Advisor	-3.08 (1.98)	-10.64* (1.94)
Public Fund	-3.62 (1.95)	-8.40* (1.93)
Private Fund	-2.85 (1.89)	-7.24* (1.87)
Guaranteed	-2.93 (1.94)	-8.82* (1.93)
Multi-Advisor	-4.16 (1.96)	-8.97* (1.97)
Single Advisor	-3.12 (1.94)	-9.33* (1.92)

Values are ADF statistics, and DW statistics in parentheses.
* Denotes significance of ADF statistic at the 1% level, from MacKinnon (1991).

We find that none of the indices are stationary, as evidenced by the small values of the ADF statistics, ranging from –4.16 to –2.85, none of which is large enough (in absolute value) to reject the hypothesis of nonstationarity at the 1 percent, 5 percent, or 10 percent significance level. However, when first differences are employed, the ADF statistics, ranging from –10.64 to –7.24, are large enough (in absolute value) to reject nonstationarity at the 1 percent level in all classes. The Durbin-Watson statistics from the original and differenced series are near 2, providing evidence of serial independence among the errors ε_t and vindicating our choice of $p=1$ in equation (2). Thus, it appears that further analyses of these data need only consider first differences to achieve stationarity, and that such analyses would likely not be exposed to dangers associated with over-differencing.

Results of the random walk test are found in Table 8.3, which presents parameter estimates for models (5) and (6) on the original series Y_t, along with corresponding standard errors in parentheses. The *F*-statistic for testing $(\alpha, \beta, \rho) = (\alpha, 0, 1)$ is presented in the last column, along with asterisks to denote significance.

We find no evidence of random walk behavior in any of the classes of managed futures; indeed, the *F*-statistics, which ranged from 4.07 in the Private Pool to 8.64 in the Multi-Advisor, were large enough to reject model (6) in favor of model (5), at the 0.05 significance level. This is especially true in the Public Fund and Multi-Advisor categories.

Even if one chooses to ignore results of the *F*-test and select model (6) as the model of choice, it is useful to determine whether this is a random walk with *drift*. Large estimated values of the drift parameter (α), coupled with small standard errors (usually an estimate more than twice as large as its standard error is required) would suggest such a pattern. Table 8.3 thus provides evidence of positive drift $(\alpha > 0)$ in all classes. However, the value of α is not large enough to attain significance in the Public Fund and Multi-Advisor categories.

SUMMARY AND CONCLUSION

These results have important ramifications for practitioners using alternative investments in their investment strategies. Managed futures will underperform stock market indices during bull markets, but outperform both indices and hedge funds during bear markets. Because of increasing volatility in global equity markets over the last few years, an increasing number of stock and bond portfolio managers, and some fund of hedge fund managers, have been allocating small portions of their assets into managed futures. Indeed, when properly used, these alternative investments are a necessity for diversification and downside protection during down markets.

The nonstationarity observed in all the indices under consideration implies that investors wishing to include managed futures as part of their investments cannot be assured that NAVs from these managed futures will be mean reverting. On the other hand, the absence of random walk behavior in all indices, coupled with evidence of positive drift, leaves open the possibility that these returns will contain discernable patterns, such as increasing trends. It stands to reason that portfolio managers holding managed futures can use historical NAVs from these series to design predictive models for future trading strategies. They should consider managed futures within categories exhibiting low volatility, such as those found in the Public and Multi-Advisor classes. By allocating assets into various commodity futures, portfolio managers could, in times of increased market volatility, add value to traditional stock, bond, and currency portfolios by providing returns that are more readily predictable. Certain fund of funds managers are aware of the advantages of managed futures, and have included them as part of their investment plans for quite some time.

Table 8.3
Parameter Estimates and Standard Errors from Equations (5) and (6), along with F-tests, for Monthly Mean Managed Futures NAVs, 1990 to 2000

Zurich Futures Advisor Sub Index		α	β	$\rho - 1$	λ_1	*F-statistic for test of* $(\alpha, \beta, \rho) = (\alpha, 0, 1)$
Offshore	Equation (5)	18.980	0.215	–0.184	–0.123	
		(5.911)	(0.068)	(0.060)	(0.091)	
	Equation (6)	1.456	—	—	–0.215	4.96 ***
		(0.428)	—	—	(0.089)	
Public Fund	Equation (5)	33.323	0.212	–0.190	0.096	
		(9.034)	(0.061)	(0.052)	(0.092)	
	Equation (6)	1.152	—	—	–0.003	6.56 ***
		(0.735)	—	—	(0.091)	
Private Pool	Equation (5)	49.729	0.805	–0.124	0.047	
		(15.739)	(0.287)	(0.043)	(0.095)	
	Equation (6)	6.79	—	—	–0.020	4.07 **
		(2.225)	—	—	(0.094)	
Guaranteed	Equation (5)	13.408	0.089	–0.124	0.095	
		(4.399)	(0.031)	(0.042)	(0.092)	
	Equation (6)	0.662	—	—	0.028	4.29 **
		(0.304)	—	—	(0.091)	
Multi–Advisor	Equation (5)	43.565	0.306	–0.246	0.107	
		(10.253)		(0.076)	(0.059)	(0.090)
	Equation (6)	1.453	—	—	–0.015	8.64 ***
		(0.783)	—	—	(0.090)	
Single Advisor	Equation (5)	39.047	0.478	–0.176	–0.135	
		(11.599)	(0.156)	(0.056)	(0.092)	
	Equation (6)	3.352	—	—	–0.227	4.86 ***
		(1.013)	—	—	(0.089)	

Values are parameter estimates from Equations (5) and (6), with corresponding standard errors in parentheses, and F-statistics. *** denotes significance at 1% level, ** at 5% level, and * at 10%

We used the monthly mean NAVs within each managed futures category in all our analyses. Using mean NAVs does not provide information on any particular futures manager, only on the overall behavior of the NAVs within each category. Thus, our results are especially useful for investors wishing to allocate holdings into a large number of different managed futures within a particular category only – in that case, mean NAVs would be an adequate summary measure of monthly performance. Futures managers do not charge commission fees, but they do receive management and performance fees. Our analyses assume no management turnover, since some funds will have lock up periods of two years. We also ran ADF test on thirty futures managers in each classification and found the results to be virtually identical when indices were used.

However, investors wishing to invest in a small number of managed futures would likely benefit from an analysis similar to this one, but using NAVs from individual futures managers instead. Given the volatility of stock markets and the growing interest in managed futures on the part of academics and practitioners, we believe that a closer look into the stochastic behavior of managed futures and other derivative instruments is warranted. Additional research would be required to ascertain whether other type of managed futures trading advisors (such as those found in the Barclay Trading Group database) follow random walks.

Appendix

To test for nonstationarity in monthly NAVs of managed futures, we use the Augmented Dickey-Fuller test (Dickey and Fuller (1981), Hamilton (1994)). This method supposes that the monthly mean futures manager NAV, Y_t, can be described by the following equation

$$Y_t = \alpha + \beta t + \rho Y_{t-1} + \sum_{j=1}^{p} \lambda_j \Delta Y_{t-j} + \varepsilon_t, \qquad (1)$$

which can be re-written as

$$Y_t - Y_{t-1} = \alpha + \beta t + (\rho - 1)Y_{t-1} + \sum_{j=1}^{p} \lambda_j \Delta Y_{t-j} + \varepsilon_t, \qquad (2)$$

where $\Delta Y_t = Y_t - Y_{t-1}$ are the *first differences*, and where the number of lags, p, is chosen sufficiently large so that the resulting error terms ε_t are serially independent. This latter condition can be verified by examining the resulting Durbin-Watson statistic; a value near 2 indicates serial independence. The ADF test works by running a regression on model (2) and calculating a t-statistic (called the tau-statistic) to test for the presence of a unit root. In other words, it tests whether the regression parameter $\rho - 1 = 0$ (or equivalently, $\rho = 1$). If the hypothesis of nonstationarity cannot be rejected, then one often performs the test using first differences: denote these as $W_t = Y_t - Y_{t-1}$, replace Y_t by W_t (and its lagged values) in equation (2) and repeat the analysis.

As explained by Pindyck and Rubinfeld (1998), to test for random walks one must suppose that Y_t in equation (2) can be described without lagged first differences

$$Y_t - Y_{t-1} = \alpha + \beta t + (\rho - 1)Y_{t-1} + \varepsilon_t, \tag{3}$$

and test whether $\beta = 0$ and $\rho = 1$ simultaneously in this equation. This determines whether Y_t instead follows a random walk with drift parameter α, sometimes referred to as a difference-stationary process (Gujarati (1995));

$$Y_t = \alpha + Y_{t-1} + \varepsilon_t. \tag{4}$$

One then runs the ADF test with p=1, so that equation (2) becomes the "unrestricted" model

$$Y_t - Y_{t-1} = \alpha + \beta t + (\rho - 1)Y_{t-1} + \lambda_1 \Delta Y_{t-1} + \varepsilon_t, \tag{5}$$

while the "restricted" model ($\beta = 0$ and $\rho = 1$) is

$$Y_t - Y_{t-1} = \alpha + \lambda_1 \Delta Y_{t-1} + \varepsilon_t. \tag{6}$$

The error sum of squares from regressions on models (5) and (6), is used to obtain an F-statistic for the test of $(\alpha, \beta, \rho) = (\alpha, 0, 1)$. Large values of the F-statistic will lead to the rejection of this hypothesis. One then concludes that the model with trend (5), rather than the random walk model with drift (6), is the model of choice. Failure to reject this hypothesis provides evidence toward random walk behavior since model (6) would be employed.

Under the null hypothesis (when the series are nonstationary), neither test statistic described above follows a F- or t-distribution, even in large samples, so in order to assess significance, the statistics must be compared to critical values tabulated by MacKinnon (1991), who updated those from Dickey and Fuller (1981).

CHAPTER 9

Do Hedge Fund Returns Follow Random Walks?

INTRODUCTION

This chapter investigates the performance of a simple trading rule applied to hedge funds. This should be of some interest to derivative specialists for two reasons. First, hedge funds are one of the principal users of derivative products and provide a great deal of liquidity in derivative markets. Second, the analysis of trading rules is also of importance, as many practitioners in derivative markets employ such rules as components of their trading and exposure decisions. In this chapter, we investigate whether monthly median returns of hedge funds follow random walks. The stochastic nature of certain financial time series, such as stock prices and market indices, is well documented – indeed, many studies have determined that such series often follow random walks, and consequently, that portfolio managers cannot ignore their behavior. Unit root tests such as the Augmented Dickey-Fuller (ADF) test can be used to identify random walk behavior in time series. Furthermore, previous evidence suggests that unit roots tests can allow for the identification of the types of shocks that move hedge fund classes (Grieb and Reyes (1999)). We believe that managers holding hedge funds in their portfolios would benefit from an investigation of the stochastic properties of hedge funds.

Many authors have concluded that research on the performance persistence of hedge funds has yielded mixed results and that the jury is still out on this issue (Agarwal and Naik (2000c); Liang (1999), Fung and Hsieh (1997); Ackermann, McEnally, and Ravenscraft (1999); Brown, Goetzmann, and Ibbotson (1999)). However, it is generally agreed that during bear markets, hedge funds have a tendency to outperform market indices such as the S&P 500 Index, but conversely, that they tend to underperform them during bull markets (Liang (1999), Edwards and Caglayan (2001b)).

Hedge funds exhibit low correlation with traditional stock, bond, and currency markets and are powerful tools for portfolio diversification (Schneeweis and Spurgin (1998a); Brorsen and Harri (1998)). Hedge funds, and funds of hedge funds, improve the risk return characteristics of institutional investment portfolios, because the dynamic trading strategies they offer are often required in constructing optimal portfolios with low volatility (Fung and Hsieh (1997)).

Agarwal and Naik (2000b) separate the different hedge fund strategies into two broad categories: "Non-Directional" and "Directional." Hedge funds with low correlation with respect to the market, such as Market Neutral, are considered non-directional and those with high correlation to the market are considered directional. The authors classify Market Neutral and Event Driven classes as being non-directional. Since we are using a different hedge fund database (Zurich/LaPorte), the remaining strategies are considered as being directional (Table 9.1).

Similar to stock and bonds, some hedge funds and funds of hedge funds are actively traded on European exchanges (such as ALTIN, which trades on the Swiss Stock exchange), thereby allowing institutional investors to shift assets into these funds at times of increased volatility. Although most hedge funds have lock-up periods of one or two years, some trade on a daily basis without lock-up periods and some even provide daily NAVs and weekly redemptions. Thus, in theory, no investor could expect to profit by following an arbitrary trading strategy, as opposed to buying and holding a hedge fund. Still, one must consider the possibility that hedge fund returns follow random walks as opposed to some discernable trend. If the returns do indeed follow random walks, then temporary shocks in the returns would tend to persist rather than dissipate by reversion to the mean level. Such behavior would likely affect the timing of asset allocation in and out of the fund.

Time series characterized by "mean reversion" is the term often used in the financial literature to describe time series known as "second-order stationary," "weak stationary," or simply "stationary," time series in the statistical literature. They possess the desirable properties of a constant mean and variance, and of autocorrelations that depend only on the time lag.

Stationary series are easier to represent over past and future time periods, by models such as the autoregressive, integrated, moving average (ARIMA) model, than nonstationary series. Nonstationarity in time series can be ascertained by testing for the presence of a unit root, using so-called *unit root tests* such as the Augmented Dickey-Fuller (ADF) test. However, if a series is found to be nonstationary by the ADF test, it does not necessarily imply that it behaves like a random walk, since random walks are but one example of nonstationary time series. Fortunately, the ADF test can also be used to test specifically for random walks in nonstationary series.

This investigation into random walks is important, because no hedge fund strategy that relies only on historical returns can be continuously profitable if securities markets are efficient and the random walk hypothesis holds true. In this case, future returns would be entirely unaffected by the historical performance (Pindyck and Rubinfeld (1998)). Many money managers today still rely on the very limited concept of correlation to examine the relationship between assets (Alexander, Giblin, and Weddington (2001)).

DATA AND METHODOLOGY

The data set consists of 1,484 offshore and onshore hedge funds that reported results to LaPorte Asset Allocation System/Zurich Capital Markets database, covering monthly returns from January 1991 to December 2000. One hundred and twenty monthly observations are used for each hedge fund class. For purposes this chapter, median returns in each hedge fund class are employed, because in the presence of highly skewed data, the median represents a more appropriate measure of central tendency than the mean. The Zurich database used in this study only examines live hedge funds, so the results will likely suffer from survivorship bias (Fung and Hsieh (1997); Brorsen and Harri (1998)). It is well documented in the mutual fund literature that daily data provide better estimates than monthly data, and help increase the power of tests (Kothari and Warner (2001); Bollen and Busse (2001)). Unfortunately, hedge fund database vendors only provide monthly data.

The Zurich database provides returns net of all fees and separates hedge fund styles into the following ten classes: Event Driven, Global International, Global Established, Global Emerging, Global Macro, Market Neutral, Fund of Hedge Funds, Short Sellers, Long Only, and Sector. For our purposes, we only examine the first eight classes, with monthly data points from January 1991 to December 2000. The Zurich/Laporte database does not provide median values for the Long Only class, while those of the Sector class begin only in 1999. Therefore, these two classes are excluded from analysis.

The Augmented Dickey-Fuller (ADF) test (Dickey and Fuller (1981), Hamilton (1994)) supposes that the monthly median hedge fund return, Y_t, can be described by the following equation

$$Y_t = \alpha + \beta t + \rho Y_{t-1} + \sum_{j=1}^{p} \lambda_j \Delta Y_{t-j} + \varepsilon_t, \tag{1}$$

which can be re-written as

$$Y_t - Y_{t-1} = \alpha + \beta t + (\rho - 1) Y_{t-1} + \sum_{j=1}^{p} \lambda_j \Delta Y_{t-j} + \varepsilon_t, \tag{2}$$

where $\Delta Y_t = Y_t - Y_{t-1}$ are the first differences, and where the number of lags, p, is chosen sufficiently large so that the resulting error terms ε_t are serially independent. This condition can be verified by examining the resulting Durbin-Watson statistic; a value near 2 indicates serial independence. The ADF test works by running a regression on model (2) and calculating a t-statistic (called the tau (τ) statistic) to test for the presence of a unit root. In other words, it tests whether the regression parameter $\rho - 1 = 0$ (or equivalently, $\rho = 1$). If the hypothesis of nonstationarity cannot be rejected, then one often performs the test using first differences: denote these as $W_t = Y_t - Y_{t-1}$, replace Y_t by W_t in equation (2) and repeat the analysis.

As explained by Pindyck and Rubinfeld (1998), to test for random walks, one must suppose that Y_t in equation (2) can be described without lagged first differences.

The ADF test works by running a regression on

$$Y_t - Y_{t-1} = \alpha + \beta t + (\rho - 1) Y_{t-1} + \varepsilon_t, \tag{3}$$

and test whether $\beta = 0$ and $\rho = 1$ simultaneously in this equation. This determines whether Y_t instead follows a random walk with drift parameter α, sometimes referred to as a difference-stationary process (DSP) (Gujarati (1995));

$$Y_t = \alpha + Y_{t-1} + \varepsilon_t. \tag{4}$$

The ADF test is then with p=1, so that equation (2) becomes the "unrestricted" model

$$Y_t - Y_{t-1} = \alpha + \beta t + (\rho - 1)Y_{t-1} + \lambda_1 \Delta Y_{t-1} + \varepsilon_t, \tag{5}$$

while the "restricted" model ($\beta = 0$ and $\rho = 1$) is

$$Y_t - Y_{t-1} = \alpha + \lambda_1 \Delta Y_{t-1} + \varepsilon_t. \tag{6}$$

The error sum of squares from regressions on models (5) and (6) are used to obtain an F-statistic for the test of $(\alpha, \beta, \rho) = (\alpha, 0, 1)$. Large values of the F-statistic will lead to the rejection of this hypothesis. One then concludes that the model with trend (5), rather than the random walk model with drift (6), is the model of choice. Failure to reject this hypothesis provides evidence toward random walk behavior.

Under the null hypothesis (when the series are nonstationary), neither test statistic described above follows a F- or t-distribution, even in large samples, so in order to assess significance, the statistics must be compared to critical values tabulated by MacKinnon (1991) who updated those from Dickey and Fuller (1981).

EMPIRICAL ANALYSIS

We used up to four lags in the eight hedge fund classes under consideration, but realized that one lag was sufficient for the ε_t to be serially independent. The results of the ADF tests (equation (2)) with p=1, on the original series and on their first differences, are presented in Table 9.1, along with values of the Durbin-Watson statistic.

We find that none of the hedge fund classes are stationary, as evidenced by the small values of the ADF statistics, ranging from !3.17 to 0.79, none of which is large enough (in absolute value) to reject the hypothesis of nonstationarity at the 1 percent, 5 percent or 10 percent significance level. However, when first differences are employed, the ADF statistics, ranging from !8.08 to !5.19, are large enough (in absolute value) to reject nonstationarity at the 1 percent level in all classes. The Durbin-Watson statistics from the original and differenced series are near 2, providing

Table 9.1
ADF Test Statistics of Nonstationarity and Durbin-Watson Statistics of Serial Correlation (Equation (2) with p=1), for Monthly Hedge Fund Median Returns (1991-2000), on Original and First-Differenced Series

	ADF Statistic (DW Statistic)	
Hedge Fund Class	Original series Y_t	First Differenced series W_t
Global Established	–1.44 (2.00)	–7.09 * (2.00)
Global Emerging	–2.02 (2.06)	–6.07 * (2.01)
Global International	–2.42 (2.06)	–6.10 * (1.98)
Global Macro	–2.61 (1.89)	–7.11 * (1.88)
Market Neutral	0.79 (1.99)	–5.19 * (1.93)
Event Driven	–1.51 (2.05)	–6.10 * (1.99)
Short Sellers	–3.17 (1.96)	–8.08 * (2.03)
Fund of Hedge Funds	–2.14 (2.01)	–6.67 * (2.00)

* Indicates significance of ADF statistic at the 1% level, from MacKinnon (1991).

evidence of serial independence among the errors ε_t and vindicating our choice of p=1 in equation (2). Thus, it appears that further analyses of these data need only consider first differences to achieve stationarity, and that such analyses would likely not be exposed to dangers associated with over-differencing.

Results of the random walk test are found in Table 9.2, which presents parameter estimates for models (5) and (6) for the original series Y_t, along with corresponding standard errors in parentheses. The F-statistic for testing $(\alpha, \beta, \rho) = (\alpha, 0, 1)$ is presented in the last column.

We find evidence of random walk behavior in all classes of hedge funds, except for the Market Neutral class, whose F-statistic of 7.51 attains significance at the 5 percent level. It is therefore possible that a trend representation exists for this series. None of the F-statistics for the other series are large enough to attain significance. Thus, all classes are better represented by equation (6), except for Market Neutral, for which equation (5) is the model of choice.

Large estimated values of the drift parameter α coupled with small standard errors would suggest that a drift may be present in the series. Table 9.2 thus provides evidence of positive drift $(\alpha > 0)$ in all classes except Global Emerging, Market Neutral, and Short Sellers. The random

Table 9.2
Parameter Estimates from Dickey-Fuller Random Walk Tests of Monthly Hedge Fund Class Median Returns (1991-2000) on Original Series

Hedge Fund Class		α	β	$\rho - 1$	λ_1	*F-statistic for test of* $(\alpha, \beta, \rho) = (\alpha, 0, 1)$
Global Established	Equation (5)	2.357	0.181	-0.034	0.123	
		(2.100)	(0.097)	(0.023)	(0.093)	
	Equation (6)	3.536	—	—	0.132	2.62
		(0.971)	—	—	(0.092)	
Global Emerging	Equation (5)	12.906	0.069	-0.049	0.259	
		(5.124)	(0.067)	(0.024)	(0.090)	
	Equation (6)	1.785	—	—	0.247	2.54
		(1.389)	—	—	(0.090)	
Global International	Equation (5)	9.003	0.197	-0.079	0.239	
		(3.327)	(0.080)	(0.032)	(0.091)	
	Equation (6)	1.932	—	—	0.203	3.07
		(0.597)	—	—	(0.091)	
Global Macro	Equation (5)	16.526	0.305	-0.114	0.068	
		(5.388)	(0.117)	(0.044)	(0.010)	
	Equation (6)	2.819	—	—	0.011	3.42
		(0.583)	—	—	(0.099)	
Market Neutral	Equation (5)	-0.209	-0.002	0.007	0.435	
		(0.830)	(0.015)	(0.009)	(0.086)	
	Equation (6)	0.707	—	—	0.616	7.51 *
		(0.155)	—	—	(0.075)	
Event Driven	Equation (5)	4.558	0.101	-0.039	0.303	
		(2.376)	(0.060)	(0.026)	(0.092)	
	Equation (6)	1.734	—	—	0.294	2.08
		(0.361)	—	—	(0.089)	
Short Sellers	Equation (5)	13.589	0.013	-0.142	0.134	
		(4.620)	(0.014)	(0.045)	(0.088)	
	Equation (6)	-0.017	—	—	0.094	5.40
		(0.482)	—	—	(0.089)	
Fund of Hedge Funds	Equation (5)	6.083	0.107	-0.058	0.246	
		(2.521)	(0.047)	(0.027)	(0.091)	
	Equation (6)	1.319	—	—	0.229	2.75
		(0.325)	—	—	(0.090)	

* Significant at the 5% level. Values in parentheses are standard errors of parameter estimates. Critical values for the F-test with n=100 are 6.49 at the 5% level and 8.73 at the 1% level, from Dickey & Fuller (1981) Table VI.

walk behavior observed in all classes of hedge funds, except Market Neutral, implies that portfolio managers wishing to include a hedge fund within a traditional stock and bond portfolio cannot be assured that their returns will be mean reverting. On the other hand, evidence of positive drifts in five of the eight hedge fund classes under consideration leaves open the possibility that these returns will contain increasing trends.

We conclude that portfolio managers wishing to obtain reliable predictions of hedge fund returns cannot always use historical data to design systematically profitable trading rules, since in most classes long-term returns are random walks and show no trend. They should instead consider hedge funds within classes employing non-directional strategies and with low volatility, such as those found in the Market Neutral class.

SUMMARY AND CONCLUSION

Our results suggest that the monthly median returns of hedge funds within the Market Neutral class (non-directional), do not behave as random walks but instead contain trends. Therefore, portfolio managers holding hedge funds in this class may employ historical returns from these series to design future trading strategies. Due to their low volatility, hedge funds in the Market Neutral class are usually less affected by severe market shocks, such as those caused by the Asian crisis of 1997 and the collapse of the Russian currency in August 1998. The Market Neutral class is unique from other non-directional classes (event driven) in that it attempts to achieve a net-zero exposure to systematic risk factors. By adding a Market Neutral hedge fund, one can considerably enhance a portfolio's risk-return tradeoff. It stands to reason that the low volatility and stable returns in this class could lead to time series that are not random walks, but instead follow identifiable trends. By allocating assets into the Market Neutral class in times of increased market volatility, portfolio managers could conceivably add value to traditional stock, bond, and currency portfolios by providing returns that are more readily predictable. Also inclusion of this style will tend to immunize portfolios against stock market movements.

Using median returns does not provide information on any particular hedge fund or fund of hedge funds in the class, only on the overall behavior of funds in each class. Thus, our results are especially useful for investors wishing to allocate holdings into a large number of hedge funds within a particular class – in that case, median returns would be an adequate measure of monthly performance. However, investors wishing to invest in a small number of funds would likely benefit from an analysis similar to this one, but that would target individual hedge funds. Survivorship bias leads to over-estimates of hedge fund returns; this would likely translate itself to over-estimated drift parameters in our analyses.

Given the inherent volatility of directional strategies of short sellers, global established, global international, global emerging, and global macro classes, additional research would be required to ascertain whether the returns from Commodity Trade Advisors (CTA) follow random walks. Since this particular group relies heavily on trading programs, providing practitioners with an insight into the stochastic nature of returns from these sometimes highly sophisticated CTA programs could enable them to better select their CTA managers.

SECTION 3

THE SELECTION PROCESS OF HEDGE FUNDS AND FUNDS OF HEDGE FUNDS

In this last Section we attempt to provide insight into the selection and monitoring of hedge funds for portfolios. In Chapter 10 we address the following questions. Can institutional investors decide on which hedge funds to choose by using a simple common trading strategy? Does historical information provide insight on possible future returns? A few studies suggest they do not. Financial theory dictates that markets are efficient and any type of trading strategy will not prevail in the long run. The study in this chapter uses a simple trading strategy to determine if selecting last year's winning hedge fund as this year's selection can outperform the markets.

In Chapter 11 we examine the returns of hedge funds and funds of hedge funds from 1994-1999 to determine whether the size of a fund affects its performance. Previous studies investigating this relationship for mutual funds have yielded mixed conclusions. Among academics, fund size is frequently cited as a deterrent to performance enhancement, especially when a substantial amount of cash is continually injected into the fund. Are hedge fund managers preoccupied with such inflows of money, and neglecting their daily trading activities as a result? Our findings suggest that the size of a hedge fund, or of a fund of hedge funds, has no impact on its performance. We believe that investors who wish to incorporate hedge funds into their portfolios should concentrate on performance measurements such as risk-adjusted return, rather than fund size.

Chapter 12 outlines the pitfalls that can occur in constructing a fund of hedge funds. For investors, the funds of hedge funds approach is the most practical way to access different hedge fund strategies. Often they will choose to apply statistical methods that are too simplistic for proper monitoring, without proper due diligence of fund personnel and activities. Constructing a fund of hedge funds is difficult, but the manager-selection process can be made easier by the use of advanced statistical methods, constant monitoring of manager investment strategies through due diligence, and a thorough review of the academic literature.

Chapter 13 outlines the benefits of including hedge funds, and funds of hedge funds, in pension fund portfolios. Due in part to their non-correlation to traditional stock markets, hedge funds are powerful tools for portfolio diversification and help to enhance returns, reduce volatility, and increase risk-adjusted returns, especially during bear markets. An allocation of 10 to 20 percent of portfolio assets into alternative investments such as hedge funds and funds of hedge funds is considered sufficient. Hedge funds typically charge a management fee of 2 percent and a performance fee of 20 percent, but also include highwater marks and hurdle rates. Hedge funds are loosely regulated and their non-transparency makes it difficult to evaluate their positions. Selecting hedge funds and funds of hedge funds can be challenging, and a number of different factors, including the size of the fund, the number of managers, and the nature of its trading strategies, must be examined for this to be done appropriately.

Finally, Chapter 14 examines a hotly debated issue, the lifetime of hedge funds. Survival analysis has been used in studies of the lifetimes of bonds, labor strikes, marketing preferences, and many other areas. We use the Product-Limit estimator, Life table method, Accelerated Failure Time Model, and the Cox Proportional Hazards models to investigate the survival times of live and dead hedge funds over a 12-year period. The analyses demonstrate that several covariates are simultaneously related to hedge fund mortality. The median (half-life) survival time of all hedge funds is found to be approximately 6 years. However, we find that the amount of millions managed, the redemption period, performance fee, leverage, monthly returns, and minimum purchase have an impact on the mortality of hedge funds. We also find that certain hedge fund classifications experience higher mortality rates than others.

CHAPTER 10

Last Year's Winning Hedge Fund as This Year's Selection: A Simple Trading Strategy

INTRODUCTION

Random walk theory suggests that technical analysis is of limited use because stock markets react to information as it becomes readily available and that whatever has previously happened is unimportant for predicting the future (Malkiel (1998)). An important matter that has been the subject of great debate in recent years is the question of whether hedge fund managers who have performed well in the past, continue to do so in the future.

If historical performance is not predictive, then it is not useful for fund selection. While there have been numerous studies demonstrating that top performing funds continue to outperform over certain periods, some have shown that investors should not expect recent strong performers to outperform in the future (Kahn and Rudd (1995)). Most investors examining hedge fund returns tend to look at past track records as a measure of how managers might perform in the future.

Hedge fund returns have been the center of attention over the last two years due to their low volatility and low correlation to traditional stock, bond and currency markets (Schneeweiss and Spurgin (1998a); Liang (1999); Gregoriou (2000); Fung and Hsieh (1997); Agarwal and Naik (2000)). Some of the literature suggests that hedge fund managers possess good security selection abilities and a majority have poor market timing skills (Gregoriou, Rouah, and Sedzro (2001); Edwards and Caglayan (2001a)). Other studies have argued that hedge fund managers are poor performers in both areas (Brown, Goetzmann, and Ibbotson (1999); Asness, Krail, and Liew (2001)).

Hedge fund tracking services, such as Managed Account Reports (MAR), investment periodicals, and web sites regularly publish top performing funds on a monthly basis. With the recent exposure during volatile markets, hedge fund returns have been much talked about in both the academic and printed media with great interest.

Do investors get lured into selecting last year's winning hedge fund as this year's selection? A large majority of hedge funds do not trade on a daily basis and many have lock-up periods up to two years to allow hedge fund managers to execute their trading strategies. Although a few hedge fund studies have limited capabilities in terms of predicting a winner in consecutive years, this paper examines returns of this strategy over a longer time frame and the return on an initial hypothetical investment.

Brown, Goetzmann and Ibbotson (1999) argue that hedge funds with outstanding returns persist in the following year. But these studies fail to account for the returns of these winning funds over a longer period. If investors can select a winning hedge fund, then over the long haul the investor's returns should be superior to that of S&P 500 or the Morgan Stanley Capital International World Index (MSCI).

Despite the problems with performance measurement, hedge funds are known for their bets on the managerial skill talent in their firm. Recent studies found that hedge funds manifest a great deal of turnover and shift portfolio weights on different assets regularly (Fung and Hsieh (1997); Brown, Goetzmann, and Park (2000)). This has led Brown, Goetzmann and Ibbotson (1999) to discover that winners follow winners in the 1991-92 and in the 1992-93 period, but during the periods of 1993-94 and 1994-95 they found that winners lose. Behavioral finance literature has also made a strong case that investors prefer to be associated with winning funds (Shefrin (1999)).

Brown, Goetzmann and Ibbotson (1999) also noted in their study that hedge fund winners repeat 50 percent of the time. A more recent study found that large hedge funds do no better than the small ones and that asset size has no impact on performance (Gregoriou and Rouah (2001)).

DATA AND METHODOLOGY

One caveat of the Brown, Goetzmann and Ibbotson (1999) study is that it fails to examine the return over a long period, adhering to buying last year's winner. Although our examination period is from 1988-1999, hedge funds have underperformed and outperformed the S&P 500 Index during this period (Edwards and Gaglayan (2000a)). How do these winning hedge funds perform years later? Does there exist a simple trading strategy able to provide superior returns than the market? (White and Miles (1999))

To prove whether winning hedge funds have a tendency to repeat their performance, the annual returns are examined (net of all fees) of the hedge fund for the year after the hedge fund was the best performer. This annual return is then compared against the return for the Morgan Stanley Capital International World Index (MSCI) and the S&P 500 Index. If the return of the winning hedge fund for the following year is higher than the return for the stock market, then adhering to this simple trading strategy can be followed to provide superior returns for investors. For this paper we employ yearly data of active onshore and offshore hedge funds, net of all fees from 1988-1999 using Zurich/LaPorte data (Laporte Asset Allocation System). We also recognize that our data contain survivorship bias.

FINDINGS

The rate of return or ROR (t) is the return the year the hedge fund was the top performer. The return of the hedge fund the following year is denoted by ROR (t+1). The MSCI and the S&P 500 ROR are the returns to the MSCI and the S&P 500 for that distinct year. The results are exhibited in Table 10.1 and indicate that the geometric average rate of return from 1989-2000 for hedge funds the year after they were the best performing hedge fund is 13.06 percent along with an arithmetic standard deviation of 55.64 percent. The geometric return to the S&P 500 is 19.14 percent with a standard deviation of 13.36 percent and for the MSCI, 13.35 percent and 13.04 percent, respectively.

For the examination period, the return of last year's winning hedge fund the following year surpasses the return of the S&P 500 the following year in 6 out of 12 years and surpasses the MSCI 7 out of 12 years. This infers that last year's top performing hedge funds continue to be winners 50 percent of the time versus the S&P 500, and 58 percent versus the

Table 10.1
Rates of Return

Year	*Best Performing Hedge Fund*	*Rate of Return ROR (t)*	*Return ROR (t + 1)*	*S&P 500 Index ROR*	*Value of $1000 Invested in Last Year's Winner*	*Value of $1000 Invested in S&P 500 Index*	*MSCI Rate of Return ROR*	*Value of $1000 Invested in MSCI*
1989	Dickstein Partners	131.28%	20.40%	16.61%	$1,204.00	$1,166.10	23.94%	$1,239.40
1990	Tiger Fund	62.23%	25.28%	31.68%	$1,508.37	$1,535.52	17.21%	$1,452.70
1991	Turnberry Capital	75.18%	89.14%	–3.12%	$2,852.93	$1,487.61	–16.51%	$1,212.86
1992	Maverick Fund USA	168.78%	29.03%	30.47%	$3,681.14	$1,940.89	18.97%	$1,442.94
1993	Berkshire Partnership	52.29%	23.59%	7.64%	$4,549.52	$2,089.17	–4.65%	$1,375.84
1994	Abernathy Appreciation 100 Strategy	147.18%	–6.29%	10.08%	$4,263.36	$2,299.76	23.14%	$1,694.21
1995	Brazvest Fund	105.11%	–40.26%	1.32%	$2,546.93	$2,330.12	5.58%	$1,788.75
1996	Hathaway Partners	180.87%	44.12%	37.59%	$3,670.64	$3,206.01	21.30%	$2,169.75
1997	Singleterry & Company	152.27%	29.24%	22.96%	$4,743.93	$3,942.11	13.99%	$2,473.30
1998	Thornhill Global Equity Fund	403.21%	–26.15%	33.38%	$3,503.39	$5,257.98	16.23%	$2,874.72
1999	St. Geme Partners	433.46%	151.39%	28.57%	$8,807.17	$6,760.19	24.79%	$3,587.36
2000	Park Place Columbia	2089.92%	–50.48%	21.03%	$4,361.31	$8,181.86	25.34%	$4,496.40
	Geometric Average Return		13.06%	19.14%			13.35%	
	Arithmetic Average Return		24.08%	19.85%			14.11%	
	Arithmetic Standard Deviation		55.64%	13.36%			13.04%	

Source: www.laportesoft.com

MSCI. This is similar to the findings in the Brown, Goetzmann and Ibbotson (1999) study. We found that no hedge fund was the best performer two consecutive years.

By investing $1,000 at the start 1989 in the best performing hedge fund of 1988 (Dickstein Partners), by the end of 1989 the $1,000 would have appreciated to $1,204. Simultaneously investing the same amount in the S&P 500 Index and the MSCI would have returned $1,166.10 and $1,239.40, respectively. If this simple trading strategy of selecting last year's winning hedge fund as this year's pick had been adhered to for twelve years, the initial investment of $1,000 would have appreciated to $4,361.31. This compares to a geometric average annual rate of return of 13.06 percent. If the $1,000 had been invested in the S&P 500 Index or the MSCI, it would have appreciated to $8,181.86 and $4,496.40, respectively, reflecting a geometric average rate of return of 19.14 percent for the S&P 500 and 13.35 percent for the MSCI.

CONCLUSION

The above results demonstrate that simply purchasing last year's winning hedge fund can not possibly be considered a trading strategy that will outperform the market. The difference between this study and that of Brown, Goetzmann and Ibbotson (1999), is that no adjustment is made for risk in our analysis. The standard deviation of the returns of the top performing hedge funds shows that hedge funds are more volatile than stock market indices. This stands to reason, since top performing funds assume more risk. However, in general it is well documented that certain hedge fund classes, on average, are generally less volatile than both mutual funds and stock market indices. Hence, the main intention of this simple trading strategy is to convey to investors that investing in hedge funds should be for the long and not the short-term.

CHAPTER 11

Large Versus Small Hedge Funds: Does Size Affect Performance?

INTRODUCTION

Previous academic studies have examined the relationship between size and performance of mutual funds, but results have been inconsistent. Some authors believe that large mutual funds outperform small ones, while others claim the opposite is true.

Some authors posit that funds need a certain size to cover their information costs effectively. Others argue that mammoth hedge funds are too large to be effectively managed. For example, as of July 1998, the two largest hedge funds were the Quantum Fund and the Tiger Fund, and both experienced lackluster performance in 1998 and 1999. In addition, Tiger Management closed down in March 2000, further vindicating, for some, the inverse relationship between size and performance.

We discuss whether managers of large hedge funds may be distracted from their trading activities by the numerous administrative duties necessary to manage such entities. We also discuss whether the size of large hedge funds (and funds of hedge funds) hurts their performance, for example, by hindering their ability to move in and out of market positions. Our study looks at simple returns to gauge performance, and also examines the relationship between asset size and two risk-adjusted measures commonly used in the financial literature: the Sharpe ratio and the Treynor ratio. We also determine whether the inverse relationship between size and performance often quoted in the mutual fund literature applies to hedge funds.

DATA AND METHODOLOGY

Our data consist of monthly returns (net of all fees) and asset size for the entire sample of hedge funds (and funds of hedge funds) from the beginning of 1994. The monthly returns of 204 hedge funds (and 72 funds of hedge funds) from 1994 to 1999 are obtained from the Zurich Hedge Fund Universe and the LaPorte Asset Allocation System, which includes live offshore and onshore funds. Funds of hedge funds – baskets of hedge funds with different strategies – possess a unique status in the hedge fund industry, so we examine them separately.

Unfortunately, our results suffer from survivorship bias, a problem recognized by database vendors and documented in the literature. Survivorship bias is the result of hedge funds ceasing to report their returns to database vendors and can occur because the operations of the fund have halted or because the fund has poor returns. It may also result because the fund manager no longer wants to attract capital, out of a fear that size could negatively impact performance.

We use 1994-1999 for the analysis because the Zurich database does not contain enough hedge funds (and funds of hedge funds) prior to 1994. Since 1994 is considered a "bad" year for hedge funds and stock markets, we believe using this time frame will make our results more pragmatic.

We calculate the geometric mean of the monthly returns of the 204 hedge funds and the 72 funds of hedge funds in our sample. The geometric mean return is used to calculate the Sharpe and Treynor ratios for each hedge fund and fund of hedge funds. In a manner analogous to the coefficient of variation (CV), we calculate the Sharpe ratio (a risk-adjusted measure) by dividing the risk-adjusted rate of return for a portfolio (using the Treasury bill rate) by the standard deviation of the holding-period returns. The Sharpe ratio, therefore, measures the net return to investors per unit of total risk (Sharpe (1966)).

The Treynor ratio is similar to the Sharpe ratio, except that the portfolio beta is used in the denominator instead of the portfolio standard deviation (Treynor (1965)). This measure provides the risk premium per unit of systematic risk. The beta is computed by regressing the holding period returns of each hedge fund (and fund of hedge funds) against corresponding returns of the S&P 500 Index and the Morgan Stanley Capital International World Index (MSCI World), with dividends fully reinvested.

The size of each hedge fund (and fund of hedge funds) is defined as the dollar amount (in millions of total assets) at the start of the investigation period (December 31, 1993). Therefore, asset size reflects "starting assets," even though the size of each fund changes over the course of our investigation period (Gallagher (1998)). We then use the coefficients of Pearson correlation and Spearman rank correlation to test for a possible relationship between hedge fund size and the following measures of performance: the geometric mean return, the Sharpe ratio, and the Treynor ratio.

RESULTS

The geometric mean monthly returns of the S&P 500 index and the MSCI with dividends reinvested are 1.76 percent and 1.36 percent, respectively. The Sharpe ratios of the S&P 500 and the MSCI (dividends reinvested) are 0.342 and 0.257, respectively, and the Treynor ratios for these two indices are 1.34 and 1.64, respectively. Table 11.1 shows the percentage of hedge funds (and funds of hedge funds) outperforming the S&P 500 and MSCI market indices in terms of unadjusted returns, Sharpe ratios, and Treynor ratios.

Our results suggest that a higher proportion of hedge funds beat these two indices than their fund of hedge funds counterparts, irrespective of the measure used (see the last row of Table 11.1).

Table 11.1
Number and Percentage of Hedge Funds and Funds of Hedge Funds Outperforming the S&P 500 and MSCI Market Indices, January 1994-December 1999

	Beat S&P 500 (Unadjusted)	*Beat MSCI (Unadjusted)*	*Beat S&P 500 (Sharpe)*	*Beat MSCI (Sharpe)*	*Beat S&P 500 (Treynor)*	*Beat MSCI (Treynor)*
Hedge Funds (n = 204)	40/204 (20%)	72/204 (35%)	44/204 (22%)	83/204 (41%)	121/204 (59%)	102/204 (50%)
Funds of Hedge Funds (n = 72)	0/72 (0%)	10/72 (14%)	8/72 (11%)	12/72 (17%)	35/72 (49%)	23/72 (32%)
p-value for Chi² Test of Proportions	0.0001	0.0006	0.0511	0.0002	0.1153	0.0081

This is easily explained, since funds of hedge funds spread the risk across many hedge fund managers with different styles, which results in lower performance, lower volatility, and higher risk-adjusted returns than hedge funds. For example, using the Sharpe ratio, we find that 41 percent of hedge funds and 17 percent of funds of hedge funds outperform the MSCI, a difference deemed statistically significant by the chi-square test of proportions (two-tailed $p = 0.0002$). Table 11.2 shows the correlation coefficients involving asset size and the various measures of performance.

Table 11.2
Correlations of Starting Asset Size and Performance for Hedge Funds and Funds of Hedge Funds, January 1994-December 1999

	Hedge Funds $n = 204$	*Funds of Hedge Funds* $n = 72$
Correlation of Geometric Mean and Asset Size	–0.010	0.100
Correlation of Sharpe Ratio and Asset Size	–0.090	–0.005
Correlation of Treynor Ratio and Asset Size	–0.017	–0.022
Rank Correlation of Sharpe and Treynor Ratios	0.417*	0.750*

We find that the correlations relating asset size and performance for the hedge funds range from –0.090 to –0.010, but none is large enough (in absolute value) to be statistically significant. The corresponding correlations for the funds of hedge funds range from –0.022 to 0.100, but again, they are not significant. On the other hand, we find evidence of positive correlation between the Sharpe and Treynor ratios, both among the hedge funds ($r = 0.417$) and the funds of hedge funds ($r = 0.750$). Both correlations are significant at the 0.05 level. These results suggest there is no linear relationship between the amount of assets in a hedge fund and its performance (and the same holds true for funds of hedge funds).

CONCLUSION

The results of this study have important ramifications for investors wishing to include hedge funds in traditional stock and bond portfolios. Our results also reaffirm the importance of taking into account risk differences, of measuring portfolio performance, and of performing other statistical analyses when selecting hedge funds and funds of hedge funds. We find no evidence of a size/performance relationship, whether the unadjusted or the adjusted measures (Sharpe and Treynor ratios) are used. We therefore conclude that the size of a hedge fund has no impact on its performance.

As funds grow in size, however, their ability to get in and out of large positions could diminish, which in turn could nullify their intended strategies. Furthermore, we also believe that size influences the risk of bankruptcy, so the returns quoted here are likely to be overestimated, as we did not account for survivorship bias. Since hedge funds use active trading and dynamic strategies, increasing the asset base of a fund undoubtedly decreases the speed of its operations, and consequently may reduce its rate of return (or alpha). In the long run, we believe further examination of large hedge fund performance over a longer period is necessary to ascertain more about how these two effects work with each other.

CHAPTER 12

Pitfalls to Avoid When Constructing A Fund of Hedge Funds

INTRODUCTION

Alternative investments such as hedge funds are becoming increasingly popular among pension funds, endowments, and institutional investors. Funds of hedge funds are usually the instrument of choice for these investors, since they provide access to various hedge fund strategies while spreading risk across a variety of hedge fund managers. Academic studies into the performance of alternative investments have demonstrated that funds of hedge funds are good diversification tools for inclusion in traditional stock and bond portfolios (Schneeweis and Spurgin (1998a)). Funds of hedge funds have experienced explosive growth over the last few years, with assets growing steadily due in part to increased volatility in global stock markets (Figure 12.1).

In constructing a fund of funds, the selection of managers is of utmost importance, since the fund's performance will depend on the performance of the managers and how well their investment strategies complement each other. This simple fact has motivated many industry professionals to offer consulting services for constructing, marketing, and selling funds of hedge funds as pre-packaged products to institutions having no internal expertise in constructing their own portfolio of hedge funds. In this paper we attempt to answer questions often encountered in constructing a fund of hedge funds. How does one select hedge fund managers, and how many? What statistical measures should be used? What constitutes an optimal portfolio of hedge funds? Is passive management better than active for a fund of hedge funds?

Figure 12.1
Funds of Hedge Funds, 1992-2001

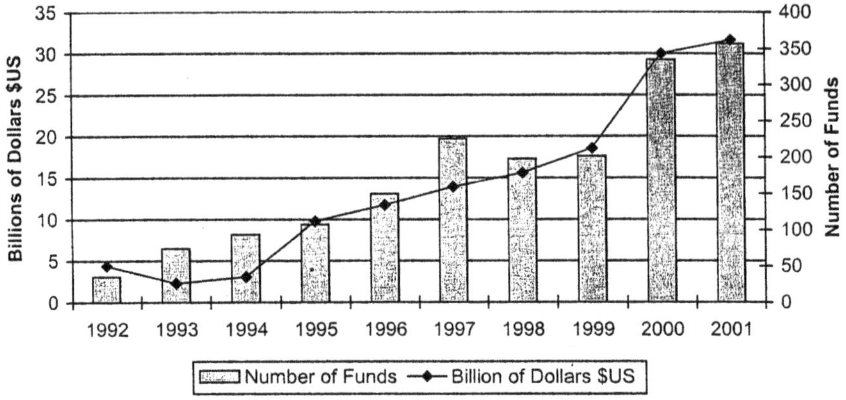

Source: Zurich Capital Markets database

STATISTICAL METHODOLOGIES

Statistical measures commonly encountered in portfolio theory include the Sharpe Ratio, Jensen's Alpha, Beta, Covariance, as well as downside measures such as the Sortino Ratio (Sortino and van de Meer (1991)). None of these measures, however, can by itself guarantee the proper selection of hedge funds for creating an optimal fund of hedge funds. Alpha and its transportability has been the latest hot topic of many hedge fund managers (Schneeweis and Spurgin (1999); Baigent (2001)). One drawback to alpha is that, through the use of leverage, it can be manipulated to enhance fund returns. Many authors advocate dividing alpha by the standard deviation, thus obtaining a more accurate estimate of alpha when a fund employs leverage. The standard deviation, widely used, is another measure whose usefulness is frequently debated (Tomlinson (1998); Nawrocki (1999)).

Other measures used today to select hedge fund managers are stress-testing and back-testing, to select hedge fund managers with low volatility and minimum drawdown, using past negative quarters of the S&P 500 as benchmarks. Mean variance analysis is also employed extensively, often by using optimizer routines (built into spreadsheet computer software) that produce optimal portfolio allocations (weights). These optimizers can, however, introduce computational errors because the iterative algorithms they employ often ignore problems inherent in any optimization process, such as specification of adequate starting values, non-uniqueness of solutions, difficulty in convergence, sensitivity to small changes in inputs, or the degrees of freedom problem. (See Nawrocki (1999); Michaud (1989); Michaud (1998)). Managers do not often consider these issues when constructing a fund of hedge funds.

Institutional investors and pension funds have stressed the importance of visiting the back offices of hedge fund managers on a bi-monthly basis to determine whether they are consistently adhering to their investment strategies. Employing all the above methods in constructing a fund of hedge funds amounts to providing a simplistic solution to a very complicated problem. One must truly understand the underlying mechanics and strategies of hedge fund managers to construct a satisfactory fund of hedge funds. Passively managing a fund of hedge funds is therefore not recommended in constantly changing market environments. Some fund of funds managers have constructed their funds using an equal weighing asset allocation, while some do not actively manage the cash portion of the fund. Neglecting certain sectors, such as emerging markets, technology, and short sellers, could result in improper diversification of the fund.

Funds of funds with a high number of hedge fund managers (>30) will find it difficult to regularly monitor those managers' investment strategies to ensure they are being adhered to. Statistical theory has demonstrated that there exists a relationship between portfolio size and variance: when more managers are added to the portfolio, the benefit of diversification drops off (Fung and Hsieh (1999); Park and Staum (1998); Statman (1987)). There is consensus among academics and practitioners that 15-20 managers in a fund of funds constitutes the adequate number in most cases. Including substantially more managers does not enhance the diversification feature of the fund of funds, as there appears to be a "threshold" value beyond which benefits are attenuated. Indeed, the inclusion of additional managers will simply increase the chance of having managers with similar investment styles or strategies in the fund, thereby diluting the effect of diversification. This is difficult to justify economically (Evans and Archer (1968); Peskin et al. (2000)). With an increasing number of hedge fund managers, qualitative analysis becomes cumbersome and requires additional personnel and staff. This may introduce a financial strain that the fund may not be able to support. Moreover, the ability to swiftly change market exposure and get in and out of positions rapidly is much easier with small funds, and difficult when there are, say, 30 to 80 managers.

Constructing a fund of hedge funds *without* a hurdle rate and a high watermark may convey to investors that the fund has low standards in terms of achieving desired returns. Many fund of hedge funds have high correlations to the S&P 500 and to the MSCI, which implies they are not Market Neutral. When examining the Zurich Capital Markets database/ LaPorte Asset Allocation System (2001) from January 1990 to September 2001, the average correlation of the diversified fund of hedge funds index was 0.39 – in line with what institutions expect when buying this type of alternative investment.

SELECTION AND MONITORING PROCESS OF HEDGE FUND MANAGERS

One popular manager-selection approach used by fund of hedge funds managers is to select well-established names ("stars") from various databases such as TASS, Zurich, and HFR, bundle them in a fund of funds, and resell it as a brand name fund to prospective clients. Selecting large and well-established hedge funds may not offer the best performance, however, since newer hedge funds often do extremely well in their first two years of operation. Diversified funds of hedge funds with a global outlook seem to be the favorite among investors (Fothergill and Coke (2001).

A recent study on hedge funds found that nearly 20 percent of the hedge funds launched each year vanish ("die") over time, making passive management of a fund of hedge funds difficult if not impossible (Brown, Goetzmann, and Park (2001)). Performing factor analysis and cointegration (especially for long/short equity hedge funds) is desirable so as to avoid including two or more managers with similar investment styles or strategies, and to ensure that the managers are not dependent on market indices (Gregoriou and Rouah (2001); Alexander (2001)). Indeed, selecting two or more fund managers when those managers follow a similar pattern and move together is not in the interest of diversification. When managing a fund of hedge funds, using statistical analyses may provide some insight as to when a hedge fund manager runs into difficulty. How does the manager of the multi-manager fund combine his managers in a coherent and sensible investment strategy? How does the manager monitor investments in terms of performance and risk? When does the manager replace one of its hedge fund managers?

The rationale for diversifying across a number of different hedge fund managers has led to demands for a methodology to construct these types of funds. Hedge fund managers with expertise in one specific area tend to introduce style biases into investor portfolios. By neutralizing this style bias through manager diversification, funds of hedge funds lower the risk inherent in single-manager strategies. Active management and monitoring of funds of hedge funds provides a good method of recognizing early warnings of impending manager underperformance or inappropriate investment strategies. For example, since October 2000, almost ten hedge funds have closed as a result of fraudulent management practices.

The process of identifying the best hedge fund managers through elaborate research is considered an art. Manager selection, or due diligence, is based on the fact that superior fund of funds managers can be identified since they generally display good stock-selection abilities under a variety of different economic conditions. But if the majority of the funds are passively managed, there is little value to be added by constructing a fund of hedge funds. The selection process requires that both qualitative and quantitative characteristics be assessed. A recent study suggests that more than 150 funds of hedge funds managers have used investigative and business intelligence practices to monitor the practices of over 150 hedge funds managers (Picerno (2001)). The study reported that 25 percent of managers investigated had trading or management practices that were deemed suspicious. Another problem with funds of hedge funds is that many are not transparent; that is, they do not divulge their positions or trading strategies to their clients. In such cases, it is difficult for the client to understand how buying into the fund can help diversify the client's stock and bond portfolio.

Quantitative analysis plays a paramount role in manager assessment. Such a method used alone, however, does not constitute an adequate foundation for predicting future performance. Qualitative analysis is also crucial, since that can help assess the environment under which the manager makes his investment decisions. It is also important that the fund of hedge funds manager demonstrate a consistent investment philosophy. A good active manager may decide to augment the risk level of the fund during good economic periods, and reduce it during bad periods.

Academic studies have suggested that hedge funds experience their best performance during their first two years of existence. A recent study on the mortality rate of hedge funds (Howell (2001)) demonstrated that fund failures peak at 28 months (Figure 12.2). These two findings imply that elimination of the fund from the portfolio after 24 months could be a wise strategy.

Figure 12.2
Incidence Failure by Age of Hedge Funds

Age (Years)	*Proportion of All Failures (%)*
1 or less	7.4
2	20.3
3	18.6
4	15.8
5	12.9
6 and above	25.1

Source: Howell, 2001, p.58

In cases where stock markets have experienced extreme market movements (such as those during market corrections), studies have found that hedge funds tend to correlate with each other, and with markets (Solnik and Longin (2001)). Over the last five and ten-year periods, many funds of hedge funds have produced dismal results, partly because of poor hedge fund manager selection and a misunderstanding of statistical measures. Managers must also be aware of the ideal number of hedge fund styles required for constructing an optimal fund of hedge funds (Gregoriou (2000)).

CONCLUSION

In this chapter we have attempted to outline some of the problems managers are likely to encounter in constructing a multi-manager hedge fund. Among the issues that need to be considered are the size of the allocation of hedge funds and managed futures in traditional portfolios, an assessment of the effect of fund size on performance, how the number of managers in a multi-manager fund affects its effectiveness as a portfolio diversifier, and how statistical measures should be used (Gregoriou and Rouah (2002)). We believe that constructing a fund of funds is difficult, but the manager selection process can be made easier by the use of appropriate statistical methods, constant monitoring of manager investment strategy, and a thorough review of the academic literature.

CHAPTER 13

The Role of Hedge Funds in Pension Fund Portfolios:

Buying Protection in Bear Markets

INTRODUCTION

Investors today seem to be mesmerized by the stellar returns of hedge funds, and continue to focus solely on expected future returns when selecting alternative investments for inclusion in their portfolios. Hedge funds provide unique risk and return opportunities, both as stand-alone investments and as diversifiers, in traditional stock and bond portfolios. Over this past decade, pension funds have been allocating an increasing amount of their assets to alternative investments, such as hedge funds and funds of hedge funds (a basket of hedge funds) to diversify their portfolios (Figure 13.1).

Figure 13.1 Number and Assets of Funds of Hedge Funds, 1992-2000

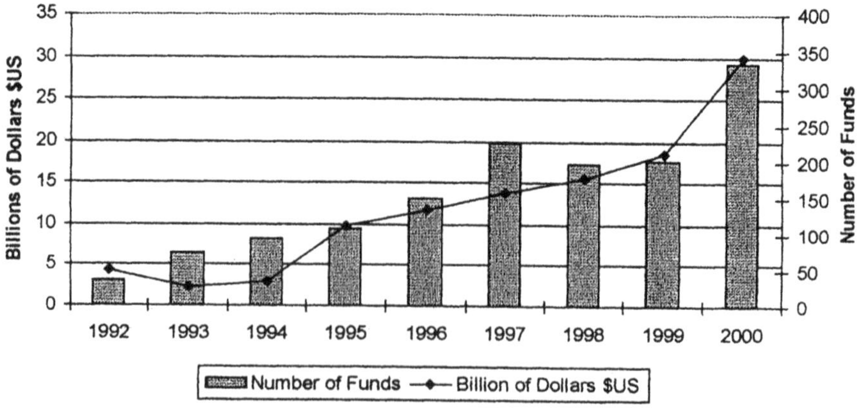

Unfortunately, institutional investors having no expertise in selecting hedge funds often choose the most established and well-known managers, rather than using a formal selection process based on research and a review of the literature. It is projected that by 2006, approximately US$1.7 trillion worldwide will be invested in hedge fund assets (Rao and Szilagyi (1998)). Hedge funds provide flexibility to move in and out of markets, making them a suitable alternative asset class for many investors. Unlike their mutual fund counterparts, hedge fund managers focus on absolute returns and their ultimate goal is to profit in all types of market environments.

LOW CORRELATION

Hedge funds provide superior risk-adjusted returns (Sharpe ratio) and low volatility, and show evidence of low correlation to traditional stock, bond, and currency markets (Schneeweis, Spurgin, and Potter (1996)). Pension fund managers often have pre-conceived notions of hedge funds as being too risky. In fact, as can be seen from Figure 13.2, hedge funds (and funds of hedge funds) have exhibited low volatility and superior performance during negative S&P 500 quarters.

Figure 13.2
Performance of Hedge Funds and Funds of Hedge Funds in Negative S&P 500 Quarters 1986-2001

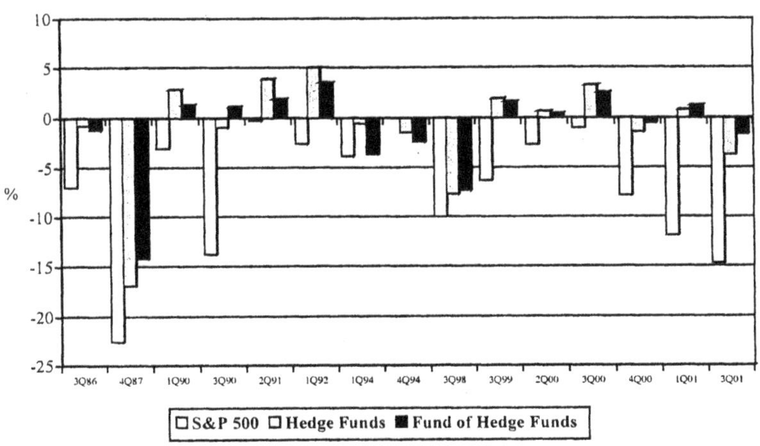

Source: MAR/LaPorte

Managers of these funds have been rewarded in recent times. A good example is the first quarter of 2001, when the S&P 500 Index experienced its worst quarter since 1987. During this period, hedge funds (and funds of hedge funds) were in positive territory, in part because of their low correlation to market indices. Many plan sponsors today employ traditional money managers, but unfortunately most of them are closet indexers and provide neither protection nor added value in extreme market movements.

IDEAL ALLOCATION IN PENSION FUND PORTFOLIOS

Some pension funds are now beginning to accept levels of 5 to 15 percent of portfolio holdings allocated in hedge funds and funds of hedge funds (Gregoriou (2000)). Endowment funds and institutional investors have embraced alternative investments with more enthusiasm than pension funds, probably due to the longer time horizon and complementary match with the liability stream of pension funds. Hedge funds usually can be redeemed on a monthly or a quarterly basis and thus are classified as investments with limited liquidity. Moreover, many hedge funds have lock-up periods, usually lasting one to two years, to allow the manager enough time to execute the different strategies driving his or her investment style.

Many endowment funds in the United States and Canada, such as those managed by Harvard University, Yale University, and the University of Toronto, have reaped the benefits offered by hedge funds (and funds of hedge funds), both as diversifiers in traditional portfolios and as tools for downside equity risk management. Over the next five years, pension funds plan to increase their allocations to alternative investments from 5 to10 percent to 10 to 20 percent, as foundations have been doing for many years (Frank Russell, Inc. and Goldman Sachs & Co. (1999)). It is therefore surprising that some pension funds fail to understand the tremendous benefits of alternative investments such as hedge funds. Investment into hedge funds need not be enormous or overbearing. Indeed, an allocation of 10 to 20 percent of alternative investments in pension fund portfolios is considered by many to be an ideal and well-balanced mix (Sharpe (1992)).

THE EFFICIENT FRONTIER

The introduction of Modern Portfolio Theory (MPT) in 1952 by Nobel laureate Harry Markowitz was the first attempt to explain the relationship between risk and return in investment portfolios. It was developed to help managers select the most efficient portfolio from a given pool of assets. Of course, the theory assumes that investors seek the least amount of risk for a given level of return. The contributions of MPT to investment theory and practice resulted in the development of a formal risk/return framework, in which statistical techniques are used in investment decisions. Simply put, MPT optimizes a portfolio of asset classes to obtain an expected rate of return with the lowest amount of risk.

One technique developed by Markowitz is the so-called "efficient frontier" for a given number of securities. Portfolios that lie along the efficient frontier provide investors with optimal risk/return characteristics, making them mean-variance efficient portfolios. As shown in Figure 13.3, the efficient frontier measures the trade-off between risk and return of traditional portfolios through the incremental additions of hedge funds. The optimal portfolio would be B, since that point represents the lowest risk with an optimal amount of hedge funds. As we move along from A to B, there is an improvement of return but with the lowest amount of risk. If we continue from B to C, we find that with the same level of risk as A, there is a higher

Figure 13.3
Efficient Frontier with Incremental Additions of Hedge Funds

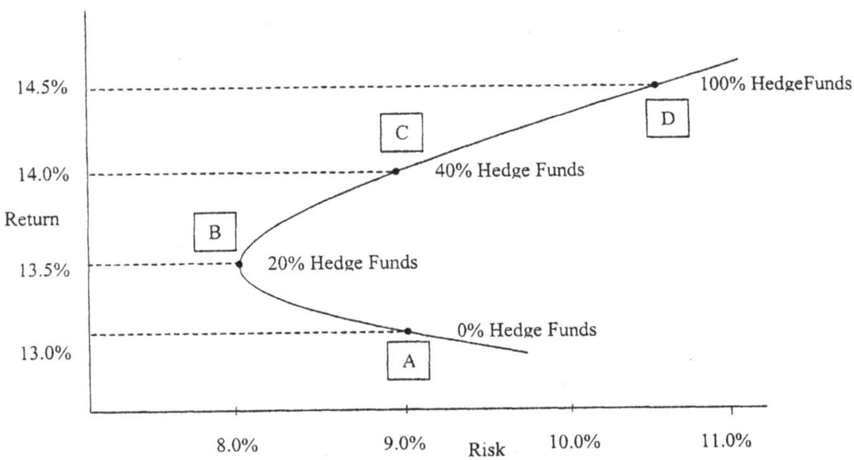

performance with a 40 percent addition of hedge funds. We then discard the bottom half of the efficient frontier (dashed line--below point B) because it is inefficient.

DOWNSIDE PROTECTION

Alternative investments such as hedge funds (and funds of hedge funds) can be profitable in both up and down markets, but their most important feature is their non-sensitivity to the globalization of stock and bond portfolios. Negative impacts resulting from the high correlation between stock and bond markets, often observed during extreme markets, are attenuated in traditional asset portfolios that incorporate hedge funds (or funds of hedge funds). Figure 13.4 displays performance measures of a typical U.S. pension fund index, compared with the same index containing hedge funds added uniformly at different levels 5 percent, 10 percent, 15 percent, and 20 percent (TASS Investment Research (1999)). The table indicates that an optimal amount of 20 percent in alternative investment improves performance and increases the Sharpe ratio, and lowers the standard deviation (risk). This is consistent with previous research which estimated that adding a hedge fund to traditional portfolios of stocks and bonds increases the Sharpe ratio of the original portfolio by between 22.7 percent and 45.4 percent (Liew (1999)).

Figure 13.4
Incremental Additions of Hedge Funds in a U.S. Pension Fund Index

	Pension Fund Index (%)	Pension Fund Index (+5%)	Pension Fund Index (+10%)	Pension Fund Index (+15%)	Pension Fund Index (+20%)
Average Annual Return (%)	13.1	13.2	13.3	13.3	1.35
Drawdown (%)	9.41	8.90	8.28	7.99	7.86
Annualized Standard Deviation (%)	8.96	8.66	8.27	7.98	7.91
Annualized Semi-Deviation (%)	6.92	6.52	6.12	5.74	5.54
Annualized Sharpe Ratio	0.90	0.95	1.00	1.05	1.10

Source: TASS Research.

FUNDS OF HEDGE FUNDS

Multi-manager funds (or funds of hedge funds as they are more commonly known) are rapidly becoming permanent fixtures in pension fund portfolios for downside equity risk management. These funds employ various trading and investing strategies and are not exposed to usual market movements, thereby providing investors with a "hedge" against market fluctuations. However, each fund of funds has its own recipe for fund and manager selection, which can yield excellent or disastrous results. The failure of Long-Term Capital Management (LTCM) in 1998 reminded investors of the importance of diversifying among different hedge fund managers. A strong force in the hedge fund industry, funds of hedge funds represent a 22 percent portion (in terms of assets) in the hedge fund universe, according to Zurich Capital Markets and the LaPorte Asset Allocation System (Figure 13.5).

Figure 13.5.
Hedge Fund Styles at December 2000
(Numbers reflect the percentages of the total number of funds)

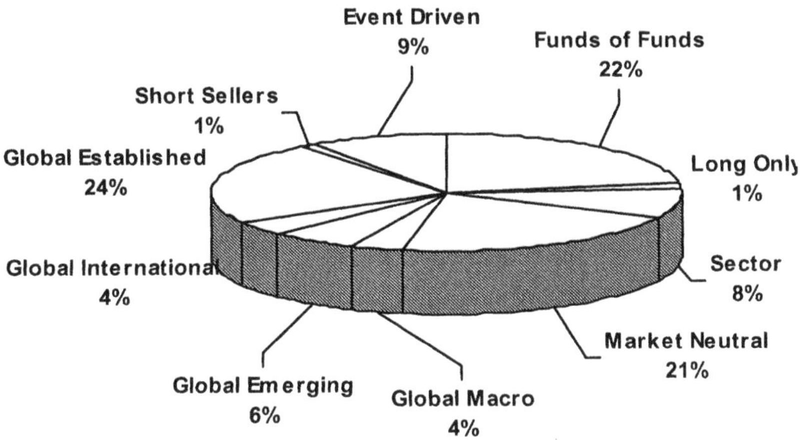

Source: MAR/LaPorte.

The drawback associated with these funds of funds is the extra layer of management and performance fees the manager charges as compensation for his knowledge and skill in selecting an ideal mix of hedge fund managers and strategies. Pension funds must examine their options carefully when selecting hedge funds for their portfolios. They must also examine the net return of all fees of funds of hedge funds, to ascertain whether or not the additional management fees associated with these funds are justified.

The cost of investing in an established fund of hedge funds can be relatively small when compared to the costs of building and maintaining a proprietary portfolio. This is especially true when one ponders the ramifications of mistakes made by novice managers. Funds of hedge funds are particularly attractive diversifiers, as they allow investors to benefit from a pool of managers who spread investment risk across a diverse range of strategies. Individually, the strategies and managers may experience significant variability in their returns, but collectively those returns tend to be stable.

There are two inherent risks in multi-manager hedge funds: style risk and manager skill risk. Style risk refers to the possibility of the hedge fund strategy not working in certain environments and conditions. For example, so-called "market-neutral" strategies are typically neutral to the direction, but not to the volatility, of markets. Manager skill risk, on the other hand, refers to the added value that the manager brings to the fund (typically measured against a benchmark market index). Non-directional strategies (such as Market Neutral) have low volatility, whereas directional strategies (such as global macro) have greater volatility (Agarwal and Naik (2000b)).

LARGE OR SMALL

Due to their lack of internal expertise in alternative investments, many institutional investors such as pension funds are opting to purchase funds of hedge funds instead of buying hedge funds directly. This is a wise choice, since selecting hedge fund managers directly (to avoid the extra layer of fees charged by funds of hedge funds) is difficult and risky, especially if the pension fund does not have the necessary skill and knowledge needed to manage these types of investments. Choosing "star" hedge fund managers with great track records is too simplistic, since past performance is not necessarily an indicator of future performance (Kahn and Rudd (1995)). However, there is little evidence to suggest that the size of a hedge fund affects its performance (Gregoriou and Rouah (2001)).

Pension fund managers must also decide on the optimal number of managers in a fund of hedge funds. As there are almost 800 funds of funds in hedge fund databases, the selection process can be long, arduous, and complex. Indeed, database vendors such as Hedge Fund Research (HFR), TASS, and Zurich Capital Market database provide monthly returns net of all fees, but the overlap of hedge fund managers between the Zurich and HFR databases is approximately 20 percent. On the surface, a multi-manager fund with 25 to 80 underlying hedge fund managers would appear to provide sufficient diversification. However, statistical theory dictates that as more managers are added to a fund, the variance of its returns is reduced by a negligible amount, while both its ability to diversify and its downside risk are actually reduced as more and more managers are added (Park and Staum (1998); Statman (1987); Evans and Archer (1968)). Prior research into this issue has found that 15 to 20 hedge fund managers is the optimal number in funds of hedge funds (Peskin et al (2000)). Other studies have suggested that anywhere from 5 to 10 managers is sufficient for diversification (Henker (1998)). Including a large number of managers in a fund of hedge funds is often mistakenly perceived as enhancing diversification (intuitively at least). The opposite is actually true, as multiple managers likely will have similar strategies, thereby diminishing the original intent of diversification.

FEES AND HURDLE RATES

Hedge funds typically charge a management fee of 2 percent along with a performance fee of 20 percent on capital appreciation, whereas funds of hedge funds usually charge a management fee of 1 to 2 percent and a performance fee of 10 percent. Most funds stipulate a "high watermark" on their performance fees, guaranteeing that, in the event of poor performance, the fee will not be charged until prior losses are recouped. Hurdle rates are meant to convey a message of confidence to investors that their fund will experience high returns — at the very least, higher than the hurdle. One recent study suggests that, among hedge funds in the Zurich Capital Markets database, those with hurdle rates have outperformed those without (Liang (2000)). The top performing funds tend to set high standards that benefit investors, whereas underperforming funds tend to select their managers poorly and are willing to accept lower fees in order to attract more clients and increase their asset base. Some multi-manager hedge funds also charge front load fees as well as management and performance fees. Hedge fund managers often have their own money invested in their funds, ensuring that their interests and those of their clients are aligned. Thus, the unique fee structure and incentive-based compensation of hedge funds are important factors driving their performance.

DRAWBACKS OF HEDGE FUNDS AND FUNDS OF HEDGE FUNDS

Hedge funds are generally not transparent. Recently, however, an increasing number of pension plan sponsors have been getting a peek into the secretive world of privately managed money. Unfortunately, there does not exist an established benchmark for hedge funds. This creates problems for institutional investors and pension fund managers alike, who wish to compare the different strategies of hedge funds. There is concern that hedge funds experiencing poor returns may accept more risk and more leverage in their future activities in order to make up their losses and to reach their high watermarks. High leverage is often a sign of impending doom, as was the case with Long-Term Capital Management in 1998 (Liang (2000)). Even in extreme market movements, the majority of hedge fund styles tend to be correlated; finding shelter under these circumstances is almost impossible (Solnik and Longin (2001)). To complicate matters further, by using sophisticated hedging techniques, some hedge funds are able to hide from their investors and lenders the amount of leverage employed in their activities (Lavinio (2000)).

Over the ten-year period from 1990 to 1999, hedge funds did not, in general, outperform the S&P 500 Index. According to the Zurich Capital Markets database and LaPorte Asset Allocation System, of the 10 hedge fund categories, only the Global Established style outperformed the S&P 500 Index during that decade. Brown, Goetzmanm and Ibbotson (1999) have observed that there are few good hedge fund managers today, and there is no evidence of performance persistence in raw returns or risk-adjusted returns, even when hedge funds are divided into their returns-based style classification. Many authors have analyzed the performance persistence of hedge funds (Brorsen and Harri (1998); Asness, et al. (2001); Ackermann, et al (1999)), but the results of their investigations are mixed and often contradictory, depending on the database and the time frame used for analysis.

The lack of regulation in the hedge fund industry is often a source of concern for potential investors. Since the Securities and Exchange Commission (SEC) does not regulate hedge funds, more pressure is being put on these funds to provide disclosure of positions. However, some have argued that increasing regulation in the United States will simply result in more hedge funds moving offshore. The added layer of front load, management, and performance fees of funds of hedge funds is sometimes wrongly perceived as being unfair and opportunistic. Hedge funds are not as efficient in bull markets as they are in bear markets. Indeed, academic studies have concluded that hedge funds tend to underperform the S&P 500 Index during bull markets (Edwards and Caglayan (2001a)).

CONCLUSION

The inclusion of hedge funds (and funds of hedge funds) in portfolios represents a unique and proven opportunity for pension funds to protect their investments in bear markets. Not surprisingly, funds of hedge funds are rapidly gaining the acceptance of pension funds. A well-balanced and constructed portfolio containing hedge funds can provide superior long-term returns with lower volatility than one without hedge funds. However, the selection process must be done carefully, and a number of issues, including the structure of management and incentive fees, the size of the fund, and the number of managers in a multi-manager fund, must be examined. If properly managed, hedge funds provide effective safeguards during market downturns and periods of increased volatility. Since hedge funds are considered illiquid investments, pension funds wishing to invest in this alternative asset class must have a long-term outlook. With increasing global market volatility since the mid 1990s, pension funds would be well advised to incorporate hedge funds in their portfolios for capital protection during market downturns.

CHAPTER 14

Hedge Fund Survival Lifetimes

INTRODUCTION

During the last decade, investors have accepted the idea of diversifying a traditional portfolio with hedge funds due to the increased volatility in stock, bond, and currency markets. One result of this has been that the number of dead hedge funds has multiplied during the same period. The unexpected August 1998 Russian ruble crisis, coupled with the collapse of the now defunct Long-Term Capital Management, claimed many victims due to the lack of liquidity in global markets as a result of the credit squeeze on hedge funds (Dowd, (1999)). Numerous studies have examined the issue of survivorship bias in hedge funds, but to our knowledge, the study of survival analysis in this area is virtually in its infancy stage. Survivorship bias is concerned with the upward bias of estimated returns that is likely to occur among studies that do not include 'defunct' hedge funds in their analyses.

Brown, Goetzmann, and Ibbotson (1999) and Fung and Hsieh (2000) found a survivorship bias of around 3 percent per year for hedge funds, whereas Ackermann, McEnally, and Ravenscraft (1999) observed it was 0.16 percent per year, while Liang (2000) and Amin and Kat (2002a) noted it was just around 2 percent. One must note that the above studies use various databases with different periods, and there exists an overlap between hedge fund managers in the HFR and TASS databases (Liang (2000)). Baquero, *et al* (2002) and Liang (2000) report that the average annual attrition rate of hedge funds was 8.6 percent and 8.3 percent, respectively, during the period 1994-1998. Over the entire sample period, Baquero, ter Horst, and Verbeek (2002) also found that surviving funds outperformed non-surviving funds by approximately 2.1 percent per year, which is similar to the findings of Fung and Hsieh (2000, 2002) and Liang (2000).

Baquero, ter Horst, and Verbeek (2002) also found that hedge fund style is a meaningful factor in explaining survival. They also struck upon the fact that large hedge funds survive longer than smaller ones, and that using leverage leads to shortened survival times, which is also confirmed by Liang (2000). However, using TASS data, Barry (2002) found little evidence that hedge fund mortality is related to leverage. In a study of bond mortality, Altman (1989) found that, as bonds age, the default rate increases.

Recent studies have examined the survivorship bias of hedge funds. The results have been mixed, owing to the different databases and time frames for the analyses. Survival analysis can partially explain factors driving survivorship bias and helps to properly comprehend fund performance. It can therefore assist institutional investors, endowments, and pension funds that require information regarding the performance of hedge funds, since factors explaining survival will also help identify sources of survivorship bias. This study differs from others in that the survival techniques encountered in biomedical research and reliability theory are applied to hedge funds.

HEDGE FUNDS AND SURVIVAL ANALYSIS

Survival analysis is not the same as survivorship bias, since the former is concerned with the analysis of lifetime data, also called failure-time data (Kalbfleisch and Prentice (1980); Lawless (1982); London (1987); Keifer (1988)). In survival studies, which are longitudinal in nature, the object is to estimate how long hedge funds are likely to survive while allowing for censoring and the dependency of survival times on covariates, such as the fund's investment style, leverage used, millions managed, monthly returns, minimum purchase, redemption period, and management and performance fees.

While survivorship bias has important ramifications when comparing returns in hedge fund databases, survival analysis provides a more thorough approach when it comes to examining the probabilities of a hedge fund dying according to certain predictor variables. This chapter will examine if hedge fund mortality can be predicted using publicly available information from database vendors. It will investigate whether the survival time of hedge funds depends on their investment style, the amount of leverage used in their investment strategies, the size of their assets, and other covariates. Each covariate will be examined separately to ascertain its individual impact on survival, and in combination to ascertain their simultaneous impact on survival time.

What are the reasons for hedge funds dying prematurely? How can these factors provide us with appropriate answers? What is the average life expectancy of hedge funds and, in particular, of each style of hedge fund? Do funds employing high leverage live longer or die a premature death? By controlling for age, this study will examine the other variables to see their impact on age. Do hedge funds that survive their infancy stage tend to be around longer? It is a difficult task to collect survival data on defunct hedge funds, due to incomplete records in the Zurich Capital Markets database; missing data make it more complex from the outset. Funds in our database may have stopped reporting due to poor performance, cessation of operations, or because the manager did not want to attract additional new capital due to capacity constraints.

LITERATURE REVIEW

No research has examined the survival times of various hedge fund classifications using the Kaplan-Meier Estimator along with the Accelerated Failure Time Model, the Life Table Method, the Cox Proportional Hazards (PH) Model, and median residual lifetimes. Using an augmented TASS database, Brown, Goetzmann, and Park (2001) observed that hedge funds have a half-life survival of 30 months or 2.5 years using the Cox PH model. They also discover young funds die faster, a finding confirmed by Amin and Kat (2002a). Howell (2001) observed that the probability of hedge funds failing in their first year was 7.4 percent, only to increase to 20.3 percent in their second year. This is common knowledge, since new funds with a small amount of assets under management will likely take on additional risk to enhance their returns and solicit investors. Rather than using their reputation, they prefer to use performance to attract investors. Brooks and Kat (2001) detect that approximately 30 percent of new hedge funds do not make it past 36 months because of poor performance. Poorly performing young funds drop out of databases at a faster rate than older funds, according to a recent study examining 3,477 live and dead funds during the period 1980-2000 (Jen, Heasman, and Boyatt (2001)).

One drawback of the Brown, Goetzmann, and Park (2001) study is that the absolute probability of failure should have been used instead of conditional failure (Boyson (2002)). Volatility and manager tenure were used as covariates. Brown, Goetzmann, and Park (2001) also found that the attrition rate in hedge funds since 1994 was approximately 15 percent per year. Furthermore, they find evidence that the probability of death increases with increasing risk, and funds with negative returns for two consecutive years have a higher risk of shutting down. Once again, they group all hedge fund styles in aggregate, rather than investigating each classification separately. Is it possible to accurately predict the death of hedge funds using survival analysis? This valuable information will enable investors to obtain a clearer picture of the survival time of various hedge fund styles.

In a recent study using TASS data, Amin and Kat (2002a) found that size and leverage have an effect on the survival of hedge funds, and discovered that more than 40 percent of hedge funds do not make it to their fifth year, thus confirming the results of Liang (2000). Boyson (2002) reaches the same conclusion and observes that hedge fund size has a strong effect on survival, in particular, that smaller hedge funds die faster than the large ones using TASS data. One possibility would have been to classify them according to non-directional or directional strategies (Agarwal and Naik (2000b)).

Using the Financial Research Management (FRM) proprietary hedge fund database, Barès, Gibson, and Gyger (2001) use the Kaplan-Meier estimator with covariates such as assets under management, beta strategies, and strategy inconsistency during the January 1994-April 1999 time frame. They also adopt fuzzy clustering to examine the style consistency and survival probability of hedge funds. On the other hand, the present study uses a combination of survival techniques to provide a longer time frame encompassing the effects of September 11th, 2001, on various hedge fund classifications. Barès, Gibson, and Gyger (2001) use a genetic algorithm and observe that optimal portfolio weights are influenced by survival rates, allowing the authors to compare multiple prediction models. They also discover that hedge fund managers cease their operations without any prior notification as a result of extreme market events from which they do not expect to recover. Boyson (2002) examined manager age, manager tenure, SAT scores, and found a negative relationship between these covariates and the likelihood of failure.

Boyson (2002), using TASS data, discovered that 57 of the 288 funds in her sample were considered dead (*i.e.*, ceased reporting to the database vendor). The author further examined the reason behind the dead funds and discovered that of the 57 dead funds, 5 had merged, 31 ceased reporting, and the remaining 21 had closed. Irrespective of the hedge fund manager's decision to stop reporting, Boyson (2002) discovered that all dead funds were underperforming and potentially would close. We also observed that of the defunct funds in the Zurich database, 531 reported they had closed, 558 stopped reporting, 62 had merged, 12 did not want to attract new capital, and for the remaining funds, the information was not available. Therefore, it can be argued that a great majority of dead funds close because of poor performance. It is assumed that few funds stop reporting because of their large size (they have reached capacity limits in terms of capital under management). Successful hedge funds with good records are frequently closed because managers have understood that size may have a negative impact on performance (Gregoriou and Rouah, (2002)).

In our study, we used survival models such as the Product-Limit estimator, the Life Table Method, the Accelerated Failure Time Model (AFT), and Cox Proportional Hazards model to estimate survival times of hedge funds. The next section describes the data and methodology, followed by a description of the models. The results of our analyses are presented next, and the ramifications of the findings are discussed in the final section.

DATA AND METHODOLOGY

The data set consist of 1,503 live and 1,273 defunct hedge funds that reported monthly performance figures net of all fees to the Zurich Capital Markets database from January 1990 to December 2001, a total of 144 months. In this study, hedge funds enter the Zurich database and remain alive until they stop reporting results for 3 consecutive months, at which time they are considered 'defunct' and are removed. However, they can re-enter the database at a certain point and backfill their unreported data (Amin and Kat (2001); Fung and Hsieh (2000); Asness, Krail, and Liew (2001)). The effect of various predictor variables, such as average mean monthly return, average millions managed, age, performance fee, management fee, leverage, redemption period, and minimum purchase, on survival is examined.

The lifetimes of funds still alive at the end of the 12-year period are right-censored since, unlike the dead funds, their lifetimes are not exactly known; they are only known to occur after the 12-year period. All ten classifications of the Zurich database are examined to obtain more informative and precise results. This should be beneficial to money managers and investors in terms of predicting death based on various covariates and money under management. Hopefully, this will clarify whether hedge fund size really has an impact on performance (Gregoriou and Rouah (2002)). When database vendors backfill the returns of funds, the data will seem to be upwardly biased. Fung and Hsieh (2000) demonstrate that this type of bias can add a yearly return of 1.4 percent. To avoid backfill bias that may be inherent in the data prior to 1993, the 1990-1992 period is dropped, and the same tests are performed with all the survival models using a shorter period 1993-2001 (free of backfill bias); virtually identical results are found.[1] Therefore the effect of backfill bias in the results is negligible. If survival can be predicted, then selecting hedge funds based on their survival times will assist in increasing future portfolio performance (Spurgin (1999); Diz (1999a, 1999b)).

ENDPOINTS

In survival studies, the endpoint is usually defined as some event that can happen only once — notably, death. In the Zurich database, defunct funds are those that stop reporting for three consecutive months to the database vendor. It is widely suspected that many of the hedge funds that stop reporting in this way have indeed ceased operations, most notably because of poor returns, but other funds are compelled to do so for other reasons. Some funds stop reporting to vendors because their asset base has reached an appropriate level and they do not wish to attract new capital. Other funds merge or get bought by larger funds or financial institutions, and others do not report because they no longer see its usefulness.

Unfortunately, this and other studies of hedge fund survival do not distinguish between funds that are truly dead and funds that simply stop reporting numbers to vendors; all are treated as deaths. In particular, those funds that are not truly dead ought to be treated as censored at the date of last report, rather than dead at that date. It is conceivable, therefore, that estimates of the survival times of hedge funds could suffer from downward bias.

CENSORING

Part what makes survival analysis unique when compared to other statistical methods is that it allows for the presence of censoring. In particular, type I censoring is observed in this study, since it follows hedge funds born from January 1990 onward, and observes their death times up to December 2001. Lifetimes of hedge funds dying within the observation period are completely known, since the time of death is known and recorded in the database. Hedge funds still alive at the end of the observation period (*i.e.*, up to December 2001) are censored, since their exact time of death is not known, but is only known to have occurred some time after December 2001. Failing to incorporate censored funds in analyses would lead to a downward bias of their survival time, since the lifetimes of censored funds also contribute information about the overall survival experience of the funds.

PRELIMINARIES AND NOTATION

The survival time T of a hedge fund is defined as a non-negative random variable (T>0), with time zero chosen as the date on which the fund enters the database. The survival function, denoted $S(t)$, is defined as the probability the fund is still alive at time t, *i.e.* $S(t) = P(T > t)$, or in other words, that its time of failure will occur after time t. The probability density of the hedge fund lifetime, denoted $f(t)$, is the unconditional probability of failure at time t, while the hazard function is denoted $\lambda(t)$, and is defined as the instantaneous (conditional) probability of the hedge fund failing, given the fund was alive up to that time, *i.e.* $\lambda(t) = f(t) / S(t)$.

The analyses will focus on estimating the survival function $S(t)$ and the hazard function $\lambda(t)$ using non-parametric univariate methods, parametric, and semi-parametric multivariate methods. Parametric methods of estimating the survival and hazard functions assume that survival times follow some particular distribution, such as the Weibull, whereas non-parametric methods require no such assumption. Univariate non-parametric methods are simple to implement, easy to interpret, and produce informative graphs, but they allow for the presence of covariates (such as redemption frequency) by stratification only — they group funds according to redemption frequency (annual, semi-annual, monthly, etc.), obtain separate estimates of survival in each group, then apply a test (such as the log-rank test) that compares survival across groups to ascertain whether or not they are the same. Stratification is feasible only when there are few strata and when the sample size is large enough to ensure there are enough funds to obtain reliable estimates of survival within each stratum. One drawback is that only one covariate can be tested at once, and groupings must be defined in some meaningful fashion when the covariate is not categorical but rather continuous (such as millions managed or leverage used). When more than one covariate needs to be considered simultaneously, separate strata for each combination of covariate levels need to be defined, which can quickly increase the number of strata and complicate the analyses.

Parametric models assume that the underlying distribution of survival times follows some specific distribution, such as a Weibull or exponential, which must be specified by the analyst. This is usually accomplished by examining a plot of the estimated hazard function and matching its shape to a particular distribution for which the hazard function is explicitly known. For example, the exponential distribution is characterized by a constant hazard, so a plot of $\lambda(t)$ versus time that is approximately flat would suggest an exponential distribution for survival times to be appropriate. The main objective of these models is to produce and compare estimates of survival times based on covariate values.

Semi-parametric models lie in between parametric and non-parametric models. The most widely used semi-parametric survival model is the Cox PH model. In order for this model to work, 'proportional hazards' between covariate levels is assumed. In this model, the hazard function is assumed to be the product of a baseline hazard (the hazard in the absence of covariates) and a term involving covariates. The main objective of the Cox PH model is not to obtain actual estimates of survival times, but rather to assess the relative impact of covariates on survival, in the form of hazard ratios derived from exponentiating beta estimates. Hazard ratios greater than one lead to decreases in survival (*i.e.*, increase in hazard). The magnitude, direction, and significance of each covariate indicates its strength (how large the effect is) and its positive or negative direction (does it decrease or increase the likelihood of survival). By constructing a baseline survival function in a manner similar to the Kaplan-Meier method, it is possible to obtain estimates of survival times from this model as well.

KAPLAN-MEIER ESTIMATOR

We use the Kaplan-Meier estimator[2] (KM) to estimate for $S(t)$ all hedge funds, and apply the Log-Rank test to compare $S(t)$ estimated of all hedge funds and within groups defined by Table 14.3 and within groups defined according to the following covariates: mean returns, performance fees, redemption period, management fees, millions managed, and leverage used. This estimator of $S(t)$ is non-parametric because a distribution for T, that is, $f(t)$, need not be specified. In calculating the PL estimator, the data are partitioned into time intervals, usually at each failure point. If r_j denotes the number of funds alive immediately preceding the jth failure (which contains d_j deaths), then $1-d_j/r_j$ represents the (conditional) probability of survival within the interval ending at the jth failure, given that the fund was alive at the beginning of the interval. Multiplying over all intervals yields the PL estimator, which is the (unconditional) probability of survival up to time t

$$S(t)=\prod_{j=1}^{m}\left(1-\frac{d_j}{r_j}\right) \text{for } t \text{ in the interval } (t_m, t_{m+1}),$$

and where m represents the number of failures.

When separate KM estimates are fit within strata defined by covariate groups, the log-rank test can be used to ascertain whether or not the estimated survival is the same in each stratum. This method produces a p-value based on the chi-squared distribution to test the null hypothesis of equal survival functions across the groups. A small p-value leads to a rejection of the null hypothesis and to the conclusion that at least one group has survival times different from the others. It is important to understand that the test does not specify which groups have different survival times, not how many. It is therefore a very general test, one that can ascertain whether any overall differences in survival exist. It cannot identify or quantify these differences in any rigorous fashion — this must be done by visual inspection or by applying a multivariate method instead.

LIFE TABLE METHOD

Another popular non-parametric univariate method of survival analysis is one based on life-table estimates of survival, also known as the actuarial method. This method is applicable when the exact times of death and censoring are not exactly known, but only available as counts within time intervals. Censored observations, such as those due to loss of follow-up, are usually assumed to occur at the mid-point of the interval. The actuarial estimator is not as accurate as the KM estimator when exact death and censoring times are known, but it is easy to interpret and convenient when survival probabilities within specific time intervals are desired.

In this study, the life table method is applied to the entire set of hedge funds, grouped into one-year intervals because yearly changes in hedge fund survival was deemed more informative than, say, monthly changes.

COX PROPORTIONAL HAZARDS MODEL

Since its introduction in 1972, the Cox Proportional Hazards (PH) regression model (Cox (1972)) has become an overwhelmingly popular tool in the analysis of censored survival data. However, some features of the Cox model may cause problems for the analyst or an interpreter of the data. They include the restrictive assumption of proportional hazards for covariate effects, and 'loss' (non-estimation) of the baseline hazard function induced by conditioning on event times.

The Cox PH model evaluates the effect of covariates to determine the magnitude and significance of these effects on hedge fund survival. For each factor (e.g. an exposure level) a predictor variable is used to describe the subjects according to the factor level to which each subject (hedge fund) belongs. The model can be used in multivariate setting to test the hypothesis that survival does not depend on the level of a covariate, while adjusting for other covariates or exposures (Kalbfleisch and Prentice (1980); Christensen (1987)).

Unlike parametric methods, which compare regression coefficients under the constraints of a given mathematical model for underlying survival times (for example, Weibull), the Cox PH does not require that the precise nature of the survival function be known nor that it be constrained by the assumption of a particular mathematical form. However, the model assumes that the hazard functions for the levels of a given factor or treatment are proportional. This assumption can be examined graphically when a formal statistical test is unavailable by examining the *cumulative hazard function*, denoted $\Lambda(t)$ and given by $\Lambda(t) = -\ln(S(t))$.

Multiple regression survival models allow for the inclusion of covariates simultaneously and without the need for stratification. We apply a version of the Proportional Hazards model (PH) due to Cox (1972), to investigate the dependency of the survival of hedge funds on covariates. This model is semi-parametric because all hedge funds have a common, arbitrary baseline hazard function. The most popular version of the Cox PH model specifies a hazard function for the ith hedge fund as

$$\lambda_i(t) = \lambda_0(t)\exp(z_i'\beta) = \lambda_0(t)\exp(z_{1i}\beta_1 + z_{2i}\beta_2 + \ldots + z_{ki}\beta_k),$$

where z_i denotes a vector of covariates of dimension k for the ith hedge fund, $\lambda_0(t)$ is the baseline hazard (the hazard in the absence of covariates, corresponding to $z = 0$) and β is a vector of regression parameters.

TESTING FOR EFFECTS OF COVARIATES

By examining covariates, the significance of the associations of these covariates with survival time will be assessed. The covariates are considered as a group, and the null hypothesis that they are not related to survival time is tested, as well as for incremental effects of sequentially including covariates. This method is particularly useful since it allows us to prescreen covariates before moving to estimate regression models.

In the Cox PH model, the ratio of the hazard functions of the ith and j^{th} hedge fund, denoted $\lambda_i(t)$ and $\lambda_j(t)$, is called the hazards ratio (HR) and is given by $\lambda_i(t)/\lambda_j(t) = \exp((z_i - z_j)'\beta)$. Note that the hazards ratio does not depend on t and is therefore constant over time.

The Cox PH model provides an estimate of the vector β, the components of which are the HRs corresponding to each covariate. When all but the rth covariate are equal, the right-hand-size of $\lambda_i(t)/\lambda_j(t)$ becomes $\exp((z_{ri} - z_{rj})\beta_r)$, so that β_r corresponds to the HR for the rth covariate.

The assumption of proportional hazards which this model depends on can be verified by examining plots of log-log survival versus time, for groups defined by various levels of the covariates. The plots ought to differ only by a constant amount over time, so that all curves should be approximately the same shape.

ACCELERATED FAILURE TIME (AFT) MODEL

The AFT model assumes a specific relationship between the survivor functions of any two hedge funds. If $S_i(t)$ is the survivor function for hedge fund i, then for any other hedge fund j, the AFT model assumes that their survival functions are related by the following equation:

$$S_i(t) = S_j(\phi_{ij} t) \text{ for all } t,$$

where ϕ_{ij} is a constant that is specific to the pair of funds (i, j). The AFT model assumes that hedge funds differ in the rate at which they age. Denoting T_i to be a random variable corresponding to the event time for the ith hedge fund in the sample, and $x_{i1,\dots,}x_{ik}$ to be the values of k covariates for that hedge fund, the ATF model can be written as

$$\log T_i = \beta_0 + \beta_1 x_{i1} + \ldots + \beta_k x_{ik} + \sigma\varepsilon_i$$

where ε_i is a random disturbance term and $\beta_0, \cdots, \beta_k, \sigma$ are parameters to be estimated (s is the *scale* parameter).

Plots based on life-tables estimates of the survival function $\hat{S}(t)$ can help distinguish between different probability distributions for the AFT model. Hence, a plot of $-\log[\hat{S}(t)]$ versus time will be linear when an exponential distribution is appropriate, but a plot of $\log[-\log \hat{S}(t)]$ versus log (time) will be linear when a Weibull distribution is appropriate. We found the Weibull distribution to be the parametric model of choice for the AFT model (plots not shown).

MEDIAN RESIDUAL LIFETIMES

In some instances the median lifetime of study units is of interest, defined simply as the 50th percentile of the survival distribution, in other words, that time t for which $S(t) = 0.5$. This is often quoted as the '50 percent survival time' in some studies, and presented with a confidence interval for this time. This confidence interval is usually based on Greenwood's formula for the estimated variance of the survival function.

Another frequently reported number is the mean residual lifetime function at age t. It is the conditional expected value of the lifetime remaining at time t (i.e., $T - t$), conditioned on survival up to time t (i.e., $T > t$), and it is given by $mrl(t) = E(T - t | T > t)$. It is generally not recommended because the mean is very sensitive to the upper tail of the distribution which is generally poorly estimated.

EMPIRICAL RESULTS

The covariates used in our study include the following: leverage, average millions managed, management fee, performance fee, minimum purchase, mean monthly returns, redemption period, and fund style. Table 14.1 displays a life-table estimate of the survival of the entire group of funds, where times of death, birth, and censoring have been grouped by year. It also displays the median residual lifetime, which is an estimate of the remaining time until a hedge fund that has survived to the beginning of the interval. A time 0 the median residual lifetime of 5.70 years is an estimation of the median time of survival of the entire hedge fund sample grouped into time intervals. Nevertheless, of the hedge funds still in existence at year 1, the median residual lifetime decreases to 5.23 years at year 2 and then decreases once again to 5.10 years at year 3. It then rises in to 5.19 years at year 4 and peaks at 5.70 years in year 5.

Plots of the estimated survival function, hazard function, and Kaplan-Meier curve appear in Figures 14.1, 14.2, and 14.3 respectively. The hazard function does not appear to be flat, indicating a non-constant hazard and suggesting that new funds struggle during the first two to three years of operation, but then establish themselves so that their risk of failure (the hazard) decreases from then on. The hazard is small for new and old funds (greater than 10 years). At its peak, the hazard function is approximately 0.15 per month. This analysis, of course, ignores any potential covariates, so we cannot identify which groups of funds are likely to survive longer than the others.

Table 14.2 highlights differences in hedge fund performance (in terms of mean monthly returns and mean monthly standard deviations). It is also found that, in the last month prior to the closing of the hedge fund, the general pattern of mean monthly returns of dead funds are lower while the general pattern of mean monthly standard deviations are higher thanthe six and 12 months prior. The majority of funds have insignificant p-values for t-test on mean monthly returns, indicating their returns for the last twelve months are zero (i.e., most do not make money or lose

Table 14.1

Life Table Survival Estimates of All Hedge Funds 1990-2001

Lifetime Interval (Lower, Upper)	*Number Failed*	*Number Censored*	*Conditional Probability of Failure*	*Conditional Probability of Failure*	*Survival*	*Failure*	*Survival Standard Error*	*Median Residual Lifetime*	*Median Standard Error*
0-1	160	317	0.0611	0.0047	1.0000	0	0	5.6992	0.1809
1-2	260	73	0.1149	0.0067	0.9389	0.0611	0.0047	5.2280	0.1573
2-3	252	172	0.1340	0.0079	0.8310	0.1690	0.0075	5.1019	0.1778
3-4	191	162	0.1306	0.0088	0.7197	0.2803	0.0092	5.1861	0.2407
4-5	154	188	0.1405	0.0105	0.6257	0.3743	0.0102	5.6987	0.4347
5-6	79	123	0.1004	0.0107	0.5378	0.4622	0.0110	–	–
6-7	76	120	0.1297	0.0139	0.4838	0.5162	0.0114	–	–
7-8	51	103	0.1280	0.0167	0.4210	0.5790	0.0120	–	–
8-9	27	85	0.1065	0.0194	0.3671	0.6329	0.0126	–	–
9-10	11	36	0.0663	0.0193	0.3280	0.6720	0.0133	–	–
10-11	10	32	0.0826	0.0250	0.3063	0.6937	0.0140	–	–
11-12	2	92	0.0412	0.0286	0.2810	0.7190	0.0149	–	–

Note: The number of hedge funds that have failed and that are censored are self-explanatory. The key column is the sixth, labeled Survival, which displays the KM estimates. At the 4-5 year period, the KM estimate is 0.63. We can say the estimated probability that a hedge fund will survive until 4 or more years is 0.63. The conditional probability of failure is an estimate of the probability that a hedge fund will die, given the fact that the fund has made it to the start of the interval. For hedge funds still alive at the 4-5 year period, the median residual lifetime is 5.70 years.

Figure 14.1
Life-Table Estimate of Survival for Hedge Funds, 1990-2001
Probability of Survival versus Time

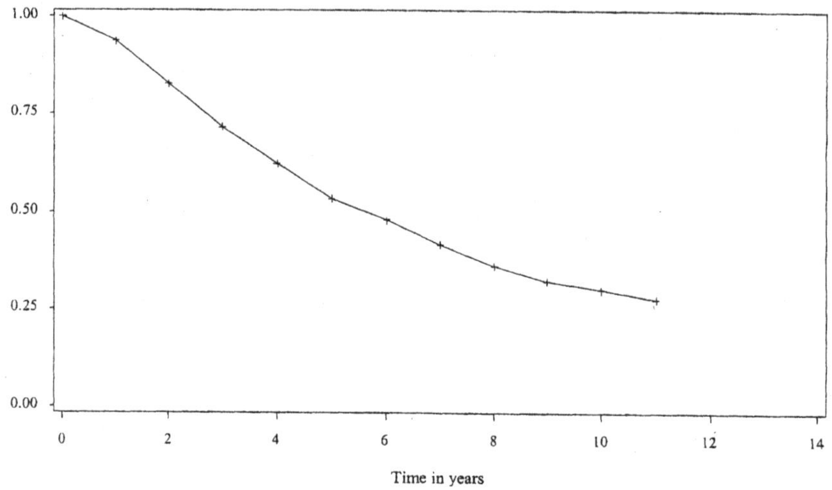

Figure 14.2
Hazard Function for Hedge Funds, 1990-2001
Estimated Hazard versus Time

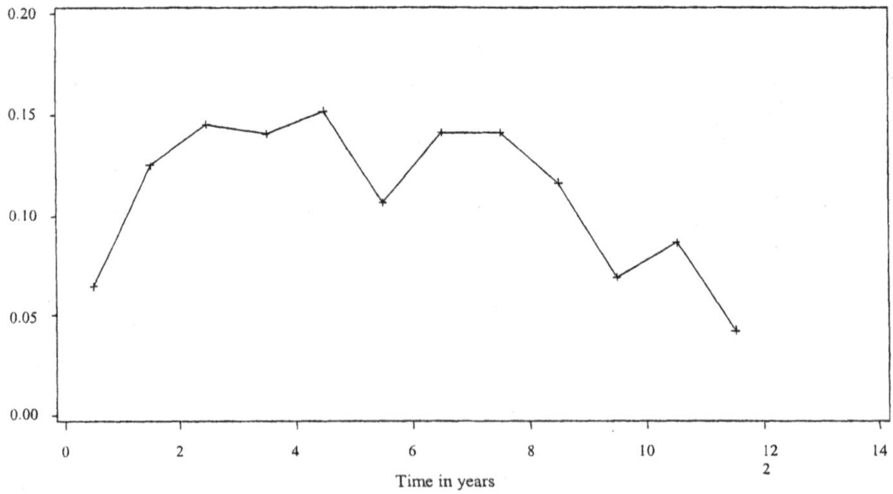

Figure 14.3
Kaplan-Meier Estimate of Survival for Hedge Funds, 1990-2001
Probability of Survival versus Time

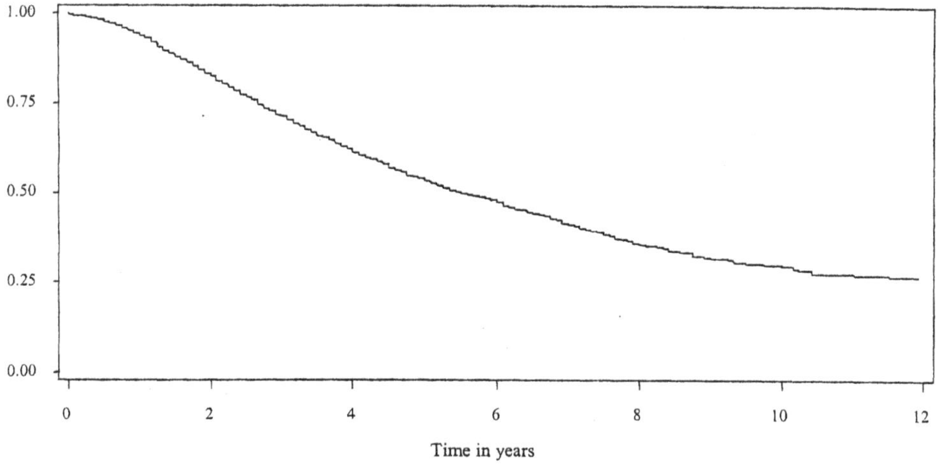

money in the last twelve months prior to closure). All significant *p*-values (<.05) correspond to negative mean monthly returns, indicating the funds are losing money in the last six months and last month prior to closure. A striking result in Table 14.2 shows that hedge funds assume a greater amount of risk in the last month of operations than six and 12 months prior to closing. The degree of risk in the final months before closing increases dramatically and the performance decreases. Live hedge funds produce returns spread around the mean, whereas dead funds possess higher mean kurtosis (Amin and Kat (2001)). It can then be concluded that that the majority of hedge funds that stop reporting to the database have poor performance.

Kaplan-Meier estimates survival time within groups defined by stratification of covariates above and below median levels. Results of log-rank tests for each covariate are presented in Table 14.3. It is found that funds with large assets (>$16 million) survive longer than funds with small assets, as do those with higher mean monthly returns (>0.81 percent), higher performance fees (>20 percent), low leverage (<1.33:1), annual redemption, and a lower minimum purchase (<$250,000).[3] No difference in survival was found, however, when grouped by management fee.

Table 14.2
Last Twelve, Six and Final Month Of Mean Monthly Return and Mean Monthly Standard Deviation by Style of Dead Funds 1990-2001

	Mean Monthly Return (p-value)			*Mean Monthly Standard Deviation*		
	Last Twelve Months	*Last Six Months*	*Final Month*	*Last Twelve Months*	*Last Six Months*	*Final Month*
Event Driven	0.4104 (.0938)	0.2473 (.4245)	-0.4228 (.2987)	2.2452	2.8574	3.7496
Fund of Hedge Funds	-0.1508 (.2408)	-0.2999 (.0576)	0.0894 (.6894)	1.9535	2.3941	3.4013
Global Emerging	-1.8696 (<.0001)	-1.4340 (.0057)	-1.6444 (.1129)	3.6550	4.2705	8.6921
Global Established	0.2362 (.3641)	-0.5369 (.1139)	-2.0448 (.0031)	4.0668	5.2965	10.6972
Global International	-0.1844 (.3984)	-0.8504 (.0072)	-3.6129 (.0016)	3.3349	4.8011	17.3038
Global Macro	-0.0483 (.8339)	-0.6748 (.0138)	-1.7872 (.0447)	2.5404	2.9820	9.7332
Long Only	0.1158 (.9068)	-0.1268 (.9385)	-3.7300 (.4097)	4.2546	7.0695	19.2631
Market Neutral	0.1390 (.2789)	-0.3943 (.0361)	-0.8774 (.0058)	2.0369	2.9770	5.0191
Sector	-0.3045 (.5422)	-2.0694 (.0013)	-1.7187 (.1071)	4.5605	5.7029	9.6711
Short Sellers	-0.7800 (1061)	-2.0192 (.0355)	-3.5319 (.0798)	2.1118	4.1033	8.7684
Average	-0.2436	-0.8158	-1.9281	3.0760	4.2454	9.6299

Note: This table provides the returns of dead funds during their last twelve, six and one months of operation. The results display that the standard deviation is higher and the performance is lower in the last month.

Table 14.3
Univariate Chi-Squares for the Log Rank Test
Kaplan-Meier Model 1990-2001

Variable	*Chi-Square*	*Pr>Chi-Square*
Average Millions Managed		
(Median $16 Million)	394.9	<.0001
Mean Monthly Return		
(Median 0.81%)	204.0	<.0001
Management Fees		
(Median 1%)	2.1	.1478
Performance Fees		
(Median 20%)	7.5	.0063
Leverage Used		
(High >1.33:1 vs. Low <=1.33:1)		
Median 1.33:1	53.0	<.0001
Annual Redemption Period		
(Annual vs. Other)	26.0	<.0001
Minimum Purchase		
(Median $250,000)	27.9	<.0001

Note: It is found that funds with large assets survive longer than funds with small assets, as do those with higher mean monthly returns, higher performance fees, low leverage, annual redemption, and a lower minimum purchase.

To investigate the relation between assets managed and survival, the proportions of live and dead hedge funds classified according to mean millions under management over the examination period indicate a higher proportion of dead funds within the smaller categories. For example, hedge funds with less than $50M under management had the greatest death rate than the rest (Table 14.4).

The 50 percent survival times by classification, along with their 9 percent confidence intervals, appear in Table 14.5. For example, in examining 50 percent survival times, the Fund of Hedge Funds classification has the highest survival time (7.50 years). The table also indicates a 50 percent survival time (median) of exactly 5.50 years, meaning that one half of all hedge funds die within 5.50 years of first reporting. Confidence intervals for each survival time are generally narrow, indicating precision in the estimated survival times, but some of the confidence intervals for 50 percent do not have an upper limit; this is due to heavy right censoring in their respective classifications.

Table 14.4
Millions Under Management Live vs. Dead Size Hedge Funds All Styles (Millions)

Millions Under Management	*Live Funds*	*Dead Funds*	*Total*
<$50	825 (47%)	935 (53%)	1760
$50-$100	238 (74%)	84 (26%)	322
$100-200	170 (78%)	49 (22%)	219
$200-$500	145 (79%)	38 (21%)	183
>$500	70 (83%)	14 (17%)	84
Total	*1448*	*1120*	*2568*

Note: The table is self explanatory and displays that a greater portion of dead funds are the ones with less than $50 million under management in the ZCM database. The total number of live and dead hedge funds is 2,776 but 194 dead funds have not reported their assets under management reducing the number funds to 2,568 for this table. *Chi-square test:* $\chi^2 = 208.8$, $df=4$, $p<.0001$

Table 14.5
Kaplan-Meier Estimated Median Survival Times (50%) by Classification

Classification	*50% rate median (years)*	*95% Confidence Interval*
Event Driven	7.25	(6.25, N/A)
Fund of Hedge Funds	7.50	(6.42, 9.92)
Global Emerging	5.17	(3.92, 6.83)
Global Established	6.83	(6.08, 8.08)
Global International	3.09	(2.75, 3.67)
Global Macro	3.59	(3.08, 4.59)
Long Only	7.25	(2.67, N/A)
Market Neutral	6.08	(5.08, 7.17)
Sector	5.34	(4.50, 6.75)
Short Sellers	5.41	(4.41, N/A)
All Hedge Funds	*5.50*	*(5.17, 6.00)*

Note: The table displays the survival rates by classification. Confidence intervals for each rate are generally narrow, indicating precision in the estimated survival times.

Table 14.6 presents the results of the AFT model with a Weibull distribution. Of the covariates under consideration, the following are found to be significantly related to the survival time of hedge funds: mean monthly return, average millions managed, amount of leverage used, and level of minimum purchase. This suggests that a Weibull distribution is more appropriate for this study than an exponential model.

Table 14.6
Accelerated Time Failure Model (AFT)
with Weibull Distribution Applied to Hedge Funds 1990-2001

Variable	*Estimate of Regression Coefficient*	*Standard Error*	*Chi-Square*	*Pr>Chi*
Intercept	2.3325	0.0717	1059.71	<.0001
Mean Monthly Return (%)	0.0689	0.0384	3.2228	0.0726
Average Millions ($)	0.0048	0.0009	31.8672	<.0001
Leverage Used	–0.0193	0.0044	18.9515	<.0001
Minimum Purchase ($M)	0.1678	0.0746	5.0658	0.0244
Scale Parameter	0.7448	0.0296	–	–

Note: All variables meet the .05 criteria for statistical significance except mean monthly return. The sign of the coefficients identify the direction of the relationship. The negative coefficient for leverage used indicates that additional leverage is associated with a faster death.

Table 14.7 presents results of fitting a Cox PH model to the hedge fund lifetime data. The results of this model are very similar to the Weibull model presented in Table 14.6, with the same covariates significantly related to survival and having a similar effect. This is not surprising, since the Weibull AFT model is a special case of the PH model. Usually, the Cox PH model is a better choice and is accepted as the standard method in many survival studies.

In the Cox model, the HR and corresponding 95 percent confidence intervals permit comparisons of survival between different levels of covariates. A HR greater than unity indicates a negative effect of the covariate on survival (that high values of the covariate lead to shorter survival times), whereas a HR less than unity indicates a "protective" effect of the covariate (that high values lead to longer survival times). In particular, as in Table 14.6, we find that high values of mean monthly returns, of millions managed, and of minimum purchase are protective, but that high leverage is not. However, the strength of these effects is varied. Confidence intervals for HR provide a range of possible values. All confidence intervals are reasonably narrow, indicating precision in the parameter estimates.

Table 14.7
Analysis of Partial (Maximum)Likelihood Estimates, All Hedge Funds 1990-2001

Variable	*Estimate of Regression Coefficient*	*Hazard Ratio*	*95% Hazard Ratio Confidence Limits*	*Pr> ChiSq*
Mean Monthly Return (%)	–0.10613	0.899	(0.813, 0.995)	.0404
Average Millions ($Millions)	–0.00617	0.994	(0.992, 0.996)	<.0001
Leverage	0.02524	1.026	(1.014, 1.038)	<.0001
Minimum Purchase ($Millions)	–0.22203	0.801	(0.658, 0.975)	0.0271

Note: A Hazard Ratio greater than one indicates a negative effect of the covariate on survival (that high values of the covariate lead to shorter survival times), whereas a Hazard ratio less than one indicates a "protective" effect of the covariate (that high values lead to longer survival times). Goodness-of-fit tests indicate a good fit of the data to the (p<.0001).

CONCLUSION

In this chapter, we investigated the survival of hedge funds over the 1990-2001 period using the Zurich Capital markets database. Our main conclusion is that investors should consider funds of hedge funds as the best choice because of the high survival times found in this classification, and also because of the benefits these can bring to traditional investment portfolios through diversification. It is also concluded that selecting large hedge funds (above the median) may also produce better results. Also, low leverage funds will survive longer when compared to high leverage funds. We find that funds with a high minimum purchase (≥ $250,000) tend to die faster than ones with a low minimum purchase. When adjusted for millions managed, however, this effect all but disappeared, indicating that differences in survival depend more on the size of the fund that on its minimum purchase (data not shown). Lastly, we observe that hedge funds with annual redemptions will tend to live longer, likely reflecting the better performance hedge fund managers can expect when they are not hampered by liquidity constraints.

Because of the right censoring of our sample (which ends in December 2001), the numbers are hard to evaluate, especially at the end of the distribution where right censoring will be the greatest. Similar to the Kaplan-Meier plot estimate of the unconditional hazard rate, the adjusted baseline hazard is the lowest for young and very old hedge funds. At its peak of four years, the baseline hazard rate is around three times higher than the levels of the young and old hedge funds in our sample.

The results indicate that an inverse U-shaped hazard function may be harmonious since hedge funds go through the learning process. Investors also go through the same learning process, opting for funds with proven track records (Jovanovic, (1979)).

Notes

1 The Zurich database was previously known as Managed Accounts Report (MAR) and commenced operations in 1993. Some of the returns of live and dead funds were backfilled. For the period pre-1993, there are only a few hedge funds in the MAR database. This does not significantly affect our results.

2 The Kaplain-Meier estimator is named in honor of those who studied its mathematical properties. It is also known as the Product-Limit estimator.

3 Large assets imply hedge funds grouped above the median of $16 million. High mean monthly return implies funds grouped above the median (greater than 0.81 percent per month). High performance refers to funds grouped above the median performance fee of 20 percent per annum. Low leverage refers to funds grouped below the median of less than 1.33:1. Annual redemption is versus all others (daily, weekly, monthly, and semi-annually). Mean minimum purchase refers to funds grouped below the median of $250,000.

BIBLIOGRAPHY

Acito, C.J., and F.P. Fisher (2002) "Fund of Hedge Funds: Rethinking Resource Requirements." *Journal of Alternative Investments*, 4(4), pp. 25-35.

Ackermann, C., R. McEnally, and D. Ravenscraft (1999) "The Performance of Hedge Funds: Risk, Return and Incentives." *Journal of Finance*, 54, pp. 833-874.

Adler, N., Friedman, L., and Z.S. Stern (2002) "Review of Ranking Methods in the Data Envelopment Analysis Context." *European Journal of Operational Research*, 14, pp. 249-265.

Admati, A., Bhattacharya, S., Pfleiderer, P., and S. Ross (1986) "On Timing and Selectivity." *Journal of Finance*, 41, pp. 715-730.

Agarwal, V., and N. Naik (2000a) "On Benchmarking of Hedge Funds with Passive and Option-Based Strategies." IFA Working Paper, London Business School.

Agarwal, V., and N. Naik (2000b) "On Taking the Alternative Route: Risks, Rewards, and Performance Persistence of Hedge Funds." *Journal of Alternative Investments*, 2(4), pp. 6-23.

Agarwal, V., and N. Naik (2000c) "Multi Period Performance Persistence Analysis of Hedge Funds." *Journal of Financial and Quantitative Analysis*, 35(3), pp. 327-343.

Alexander, C., Giblin, I., and W. Weddington (2001) "Cointegration and Asset Allocation: A New Active Hedge Fund Strategy." Presentation at the INQUIRE Europe/UK Conference, Brighton, UK, March 2001.

Alexander, C. (2001) *Market Models*, John Wiley and Sons, New York, NY.

Alexander, C. (1999) "Optimal Hedging Using Cointegration." *Philosophical Transactions of the Royal Society*, London, England, Series A357, pp. 2039-2058.

Altman, E.I. (1989) "Measuring Corporate Bond Mortality and Performance," *Journal of Finance*, XLIV, 4, pp. 909-922.

Amenc, N., and L. Martellini (2002) "The Brave New World of Hedge Fund Indexes." Working Paper, University of Southern California.

Amin, G.S., and H. Kat (2002a) "Welcome to the Dark Side: Hedge Fund Attrition and Survivorship Bias Over the Period 1994-2001." Working Paper, ISMA Centre, University of Reading, UK.

Amin, G.S., and H. Kat (2002b) "Portfolios of Hedge Funds." Working Paper, ISMA Centre, University of Reading, UK.

Amin, G.S., and H. Kat (2001) "Hedge Fund Performance 1990-2000: Do The Money Machines Really Add Value?" Working Paper, ISMA Centre, University of Reading, UK.

Andersen, P.N., and N.C. Petersen (1993) "A Procedure for Ranking Efficient Units in Data Envelopment Analysis." *Management Science,* 39(1), pp. 1261-1264.

Anson, M. (2000) "Selecting a Hedge Fund Manager." *The Journal of Wealth Management,* 3(3), pp. 45-52.

Asness, C., R. Krail, and J. Liew (2001) "Do Hedge Funds Hedge?" *Journal of Portfolio Management,* 28(1), pp. 6-19.

Baigent, G.G. (2001) "Is There Alpha?" *Journal of Alternative Investments,* 3(4), pp. 65-67.

Baily, M.N., Farrell, D., and S. Lund (2000) "The Color of Hot Money." *Foreign Affairs,* 79(2), pp. 99-109.

Banker, R.D., Charnes, A., and W.W. Cooper (1984) "Some Models for Estimating Technical and Scale Inefficiencies in Data Envelopment Analysis." *Management Science,* 30(9), pp. 1078-1092.

Banz, R.W. (1981) "The Relationship Between Return and Market Value of Common Stocks." *Journal of Financial Economics,* 9, pp. 3-18.

Barry, R. (2002) "A Walk Through the Graveyard." Working Paper, Maquarie University, Applied Finance Center, New South Wales, Australia.

Baquero, H., ter Horst J., and M. Verbeek (2002) "Survival, Look-Ahead Bias and the Performance of Hedge Funds." Working Paper, Erasmus University, and Tilburg University, The Netherlands.

Barès, P.A., Gibson, R., and S. Gyger (2001) "Style Consistency and Survival Probability in the Hedge Fund Industry." Working Paper, Swiss Federal Institute of Technology, and University of Zurich.

Barr, R., Seiford, L., and T. Siems (1994) "Forecasting Bank Failure: A Non-Parametric Frontier Estimation Approach." *Recherches Economiques de Louvain,* 60(4), pp. 417-429.

Basso, A., and S. Funari (2001) "A Data Envelopment Analysis Approach to Measure the Mutual Fund Performance." *European Journal of Operational Research*, 135(3), pp. 477-492.

Bollen, N., and J. Busse (2001) "On the Timing Ability of Mutual Fund Managers." *Journal of Finance*, 56, pp. 1075-1094.

Bowlin, W.F. (1998) "Measuring Performance: An Introduction to Data Envelopment Analysis (DEA)." *Journal of Cost Analysis*, 3, pp. 3-28.

Boyson, N. (2002) "How Are Hedge Fund Manager Characteristics Related to Performance, Volatility and Survival." Working Paper, Ohio State University.

Brealey, R.A., and E. Kaplanis (2001) "Hedge Funds and Financial Stability: An Analysis of Their Factor Exposures," *International Finance*, 4 (2), pp. 161-187.

Brooks, C., and H. Kat (2001) "The Statistical Properties of Hedge Fund Index Returns and Their Implications for Investors." Working Paper, ISMA Centre, University of Reading, UK.

Brorsen, W., and A. Harri (1998) "Performance Persistence of Hedge Funds." Working Paper, Oklahoma State University.

Brorsen, B.W., and S.H. Irwin (1987) "Futures Funds and Price Volatility." *Review of Futures Markets*, 6(2), pp.118-135.

Brorsen, B.W., and S.H. Irwin (1985) "Examination of Commodity Fund Performance." *Review of Research in Futures Markets*, 1, pp. 84-94.

Brown, S.J., Goetzmann, W.N., and R. Ibbotson (1999) "Offshore Hedge Funds: Survival and Performance 1989-1995." *Journal of Business*, 72, pp. 91-117.

Brown, S.J., Goetzmann, W.N., Ibbotson, R. and S. Ross (1992) "Survivorship Bias in Performance Studies." *Review of Financial Studies*, 5, pp. 553-580.

Brown, S.J., Goetzmann, W.N., and J.M. Park (2001) "Careers and Survival: Competition and Risk in the Hedge Fund and CTA Industry." *Journal of Finance*, 56(5), pp. 1869-1886.

Brown, S.J., Goetzmann, W.N., and J.M. Park (2000) "Hedge Funds and the Asian Currency Crisis." *Journal of Portfolio Management*, 26(4), pp. 95-101.

Brunel, J.L.P. (2002) "Absolute Return Strategies Revisited." *The Journal of Wealth Management*, 4(4), pp. 63-75.

Brunel, J.L.P. (1999) "The Role of Alternative Assets in Tax-Efficient Portfolio Construction." *The Journal of Wealth Management*, 4(4), pp. 9-26.

Caldwell, C., and T. Kirkpatrick (1995) *A Primer on Hedge Funds*. Lookout Mountain Capital, Inc., Chattanooga, TN.

Chadha, B., and A. Jansen (1998) "The Hedge Fund Industry: Structure, Size and Performance." Chapter 3 in B. Eichengreen, D. Mathieson, B. Chadha, A. Jansen, L.Kodres and S. Sharma (Eds.) *Hedge Funds and Financial Dynamics*, International Monetary Fund, Washington, D.C., pp. 27-41.

Chang, E. C., and W. G. Lewellen (1985) "An Arbitrage Pricing Approach to Evaluating Pricing Theory: A New Framework for Analysis." *Journal of Financial Economics*, 7, pp. 381-390.

Charnes, A., and W.W. Cooper (1985) "Preface to Topics in Data Envelopment Analysis." *Annals of Operations Research*, 2, pp. 59-94.

Charnes, A., Cooper, W.W., and E. Rhodes (1981) "Evaluating Program and Managerial Efficiency: An Application of Data Envelopment Analysis to Program Follow Through." *Management Science*, 27(6), pp. 668-697.

Charnes, A., Cooper, W.W., and E. Rhodes (1978) "Measuring the Efficiency of Decision Making Units." *European Journal of Operational Research*, 2(6), pp. 429-444.

Chen, Z., and P. Knez (1996) "Portfolio Performance Measurement: Theory and Applications." *Review of Financial Studies*, 9(2), pp. 507-551.

Christensen, E. (1987) "Multivariate Survival Analysis Using Cox's Regression Model." *Hepatology*, 7, pp. 1346-1358.

Clair, C. (2000) "Concerns VaR may be a Double-Edged Sword." *Pensions and Investments*, 29(3), pp. 14-15.

Clow, R. (2002) "Pensions Maintain Flows into Alternative Assets." *Financial Times of London*, London, UK.

Cox, D.R. (1972) "Regression Models and Life Tables." *Journal of the Royal Statistical Society*, Series B, 34(2), pp.187-220.

Cumby, R.E., and J.D. Glen (1990) "Evaluating the Performance of International Mutual Funds." *Journal of Finance*, 45(2), pp. 497-522.

da Costa, A. (2001) *Fund of Funds and Absolute Returns*. Vector Asset Management, New York.

Dalhquist, M., and C. Harvey (2001) "Global Tactical Asset Allocation." *Emerging Markets Quarterly*, 5(1), pp.6-14.

Daniel, K., Grinblatt, M., Titman, S., and R. Wermers (1997) "Measuring

Mutual Fund Performance with Characteristics-Based Benchmarks." *Journal of Finance*, 52, pp. 1035-1058.

Davidson R., and J. MacKinnon (1993) *Estimation and Inference in Econometrics*. Oxford University Press, New York.

deBrouwer, G. (2001) *Hedge Funds in Emerging Markets*. Cambridge, England: Cambridge University Press.

Dellva, W.L., DeMaskey, A.L., and C.A. Smith (2001) "Selectivity and Market Timing Performance of Fidelity Sector Mutual Funds." *The Financial Review*, 36, pp. 39-54.

Dickey, D., and W. Fuller (1981) "The Likelihood Ratio Statistics for Autoregressive Time Series with a Unit Root." *Econometrica*, 49, pp. 1057-1072.

Diz, F. (2001) "Are Investors Over-Invested in Equities?" *Derivatives Quarterly*, 7(3), pp. 59-62.

Diz, F. (1999a) "How Do CTAs' Return Distribution Characteristics Affect Their Likelihood of Survival?" *The Journal of Alternative Investments*, 2(2), pp. 37-41.

Diz, F. (1999b) "Survivor and Nonsurvivor: An Analysis of Relative Performance" *The Journal of Alternative Investments*, 2(1), pp. 57-71.

Dowd, K. (1999) "Too Big to Fail: Long-Term Capital Management and the Federal Reserve." Cato Institute Briefing paper, Washington, D.C.

Doyle, J., and R. Green (1994) "Efficiency and Cross Efficiency in DEA: Derivations, Meanings and the Uses." *Journal of the Operational Research Society*, 45(5), pp. 567-578.

Doyle, J., and R. Green (1991) "Comparing Products Using Data Envelopment Analysis." O*mega*, 47(19), pp. 631-638.

Edwards, F. (1999) "Do Hedge Funds Have a Future?" *The Journal of Alternative Investments*, 2(2), pp. 63-68.

Edwards, F., and M.O. Caglayan (2001a) "Hedge Fund Performance and Manager Skill." *Journal of Futures Markets*, 21(11), pp. 1003-1028.

Edwards, F., and M.O. Caglayan (2001b) "Hedge Fund and Commodity Fund Investment Styles in Bull and Bear Markets." *Journal of Portfolio Management*, 27(4), pp. 97-108.

Edwards, F., and A.C. Ma (1988) "Commodity Fund Performance: Is the Information Contained in Fund Prospectuses Useful?" *Journal of Futures Markets*, 8(5), pp. 589-616.

Elton, E.J., Gruber, M.J., Das, S., and M. Hlavka (1993) "Efficiency with

Costly Information: A Re-Interpretation of Evidence from Managed Portfolios." *Review of Financial Studies*, 6, pp. 1-21.

Elton, E.J., Gruber, M.J., and K. Rentzler (1987) "Professionally Managed, Publicly Traded Commodity Funds." *Journal of Business*, 6(1), pp. 177-199.

Evans, J.L., and S.H. Archer (1968) "Diversification and the Reduction Dispersion: An Empirical Analysis." *Journal of Finance*, 23(2), pp. 761-767.

Fama, E. (1972) "Components of Investment Performance." *Journal of Finance*, 27(3), pp. 551-567.

Farrell, M.J. (1957) "The Measurement of Productive Efficiency." *The Journal of the Operational and Research Society*, A120, pp. 253-281.

Ferson, W., Becker, C., Myers, D. and M. Schill (1997) "Conditional Market Timing with Benchmark Investors." *Journal of Finance*, 52(3), pp. 1028-1049.

Ferson, W., Christopherson, J.A. and D.A. Glassman (1998) "Conditional Measures of Performance and Persistence for Pension Funds." In *Research in Finance*, vol. 16, JAI Press, Stanford, CT, pp. 1-46.

Ferson, W., and R. Schadt (1996) "Measuring Fund Strategy and Performance in Changing Economic Conditions." *Journal of Finance*, 51, pp. 425-461.

Ferson, W., and V.A. Warther (1996) "Evaluating Fund Performance in a Dynamic Market." *Financial Analysts Journal*, 52(6), pp. 20-28.

Fothergill, M., and C. Coke (2001) "Funds of Hedge Funds: An Introduction to Multi-Manager Funds." *Journal of Alternative Investments*, 4(2), pp. 7-16.

Frank Russell, Inc. (2001) http://www.russell.com

Frank Russell, Inc., and Goldman Sachs & Co. (1999) *Report on Alternative Investing*, New York.

Fung, W., and D. Hsieh (2002) "Benchmarks of Hedge Fund Performance: Information Content and Measurement Biases." *Financial Analyst Journal*, 58, pp. 22-34.

Fung, W., and D.Hsieh (2000) "Performance Characteristics of Hedge Funds and Commodity Funds: Natural vs. Spurious Biases." *Journal of Financial and Quantitative Analysis*, 35(3), pp. 291-307.

Fung, W., and D. Hsieh (1999) "A Primer on Hedge Funds." *Journal of Empirical Finance*, 6, pp. 309-331.

Fung, W., and D. Hsieh (1997) "Empirical Characteristics of Dynamic

Trading Strategies: The Case of Hedge Funds." *Review of Financial Studies*, 10, pp. 275-302.

Gallagher, T.J. (1998) "Mutual Fund Size and Risk Adjusted Performance." *Illinois Business Review*, 45(5), pp. 11-14.

Georgiev, G. (2001) "Benefits of Commodity Investments." CISDM Working Paper Series, University of Massachusetts.

Ghosh, A., Saidi, R., and K.H. Johnson (1999) "Who Moves the Asia Pacific Stock Markets-US or Japan? Empirical Evidence Based on the Theory of Cointegration." *The Financial Review*, 34, pp. 159-170.

Goetzmann, W.N., Ingersoll Jr., J., and Z. Ivkovic (2000) "Monthly Measurement of Daily Timers." *Journal of Financial and Quantitative Analysis*, 35, pp. 257-290.

Golany, B., and Y.A. Roll (1994) "Incorporating Standards Via Data Envelopment Analysis." In Charnes, A., Cooper, W.W., Levin, A.Y., and L. Seiford (Eds.) *Data Envelopment Analysis: Theory, Methodology and Applications*. Kluwer Academic Publications, Norwell, MA.

Gregoriou, G.N. (2002) "Hedge Fund Survival Lifetimes." *Journal of Asset Management*, 3(3), pp. 237-252.

Gregoriou, G.N. (2000) "Funds of Funds: When More Definitely Means Less." *Canadian Business Economics Journal*, 8(2), pp. 83-85.

Gregoriou, G.N., and F. Rouah (2002) "The Role of Hedge Funds in Pension Fund Portfolios: Buying Protection in Down Markets." *Journal of Pensions Management*, 7(3), pp. 237-245.

Gregoriou, G.N., and F. Rouah (2001) "Is Size a Factor in Hedge Fund Performance?" *Derivatives Use, Trading and Regulation*, 7(4), pp. 301-305.

Gregoriou, G.N., Rouah, F., and K. Sedzro (2002) "On the Market Timing of Hedge Fund Managers." *Journal of Wealth Management*, 5(1), pp. 26-38.

Gregoriou, G.N., Rouah, F., and K. Sedzro (2001) "Do Hedge Fund Returns Follow Random Walks." *Derivatives Use, Trading and Regulation*, 7(3), pp. 241-250.

Grieb, T., and M.G. Reyes (1999) "Random Walk Tests for Latin American Equity Indices and Individual Firms." *The Journal of Financial Research*, 22(4), pp. 371-383.

Grinblatt, M., and S. Titman (1994) "The Evaluation of Mutual Fund

Performance: An Analysis of Quarterly Portfolio Holdings." Working Paper, University of California, Los Angeles.

Grinblatt, M., and S. Titman (1989) "Mutual Fund Performance: An Analysis of Quarterly Portfolio Holdings." *Journal of Business*, 62(3), pp. 393-416.

Gujarati, D.N. (1995) *Basic Econometrics*. McGraw-Hill, New York.

Hamilton, J.D. (1994) *Time Series Analysis*. Princeton University Press, Princeton, NJ.

Henker, T. (1998) "Naïve Diversification for Hedge Funds." *Journal of Alternative Investments*, 1(3), pp. 33-38.

Harvey, C.R., and J.R. Graham (1996) "Market Timing Ability and Volatility Implied in Investment Newsletters' Asset Allocation Recommendations." *Journal of Financial Economics*, pp. 397-422.

Henriksson, R. (1984) "Market Timing and Mutual Fund Performance: An Empirical Investigation." *Journal of Business*, 57, pp. 73-96.

Henriksson, R., and R. Merton (1981) "On Market Timing and Investment Performance II: Statistical Procedures for Evaluating Forecasting Skills." *Journal of Business*, 54, pp. 513-534.

Howell, M.J. (2001) "Fund Age and Performance." *Journal of Alternative Investments*, 4(2), pp. 57-60.

Ineichen, A. (2002) "Funds of Hedge Funds: Industry Overview." *Journal of Wealth Management*, 4(4), pp. 47-62.

Ineichen, A. (2001) "The Alpha in Funds of Hedge Funds." *Journal of Wealth Management*, 5(1), pp. 8-25.

Irwin, S., and D. Landa (1987) "Real Estate, Futures and Gold as Portfolio Assets." *Journal of Portfolio Management*, 13(2), pp. 29-34.

Irwin, S., Krukemyer, T., and C.R. Zulauf (1992) "Are Public Commodity Funds a Good Investment?" in C. Peters (Ed.) *Managed Futures*, Probus Publishing, Chicago, pp.405-433.

Irwin, S., Zulauf, C.R., and B. Ward (1994) "The Predictability of Managed Futures Returns." *Journal of Derivatives*, 2(2), pp. 20-27.

Jagannathan, R., and R. Korajczyk (1986) "Assessing the Market Timing Performance of Managed Portfolios." *Journal of Business*, 59, pp. 217-235.

Janjigian, V., and Z. Bello (1997) "A Reexamination of the Market-Timing and Security-Selection Performance of Mutual Funds." *Financial Analysts Journal*, 53(5), pp. 24-30.

Jen, P., Heasman, C., and Boyatt, K. (2001) "Alternative Asset Strategies:

Early Performance in Hedge Fund Managers." Lazard Asset Management, New York. http://www.aima.org.

Jensen, M. (1968) "Problems in the Selection of Security Portfolios: The Performance of Mutual Funds in the period 1945-1964." *Journal of Finance*, 23(2), pp. 389-419.

Jorion, P. (2000) "Risk Management Lessons from Long-Term Capital Management." *European Financial Management*, 6, pp. 277-300.

Jovanovic, B. (1979) "On the Determination of Public Debt." *Journal of Political Economy*, 87, pp. 972-990.

Kahn, R.N., and A. Rudd (1995) "Does Historical Performance Predict Future Performance?" *Financial Analysts Journal*, 51, pp. 43-52.

Kalbfleisch, J.D., and R.L. Prentice (1980) *The Statistical Analysis of Failure Time Data*. John Wiley & Sons, New York.

Karavas, V. (2000) "Alternative Investments in the Institutional Portfolio." *Journal of Alternative Investments*, 3(3), pp. 11-26.

Kasa, K. (1992) "Common Stochastic Trends in International Stock Markets." *Journal of Monetary Economics*, 29, pp. 95-124.

Kazemi, H. (1996) "The Stability of Variance and Return Forecasts: A Monte Carlo Simulation." CISDM Working Paper Series, University of Massachusetts.

Keifer, N.M. (1988) "Economic Duration Data and Hazard Functions." *Journal of Economic Literature*, XXVI, pp. 646-679.

Kon, S. (1983) "The Market-Timing Performance of Mutual Fund Managers." *Journal of Business*, 56, pp. 323-347.

Kon, S., and F.C. Chen (1979) "The Investment Performance of Mutual Funds: An Empirical Investigation of Timing, Selectivity and Market Efficiency." *Journal of Business*, 52, pp. 263-290.

Kothari, S.P., and J. Warner (2001) "Evaluating Mutual Fund Performance." *Journal of Finance*, 56, pp. 1985-2010.

Lamm, Jr., R.M. (1999) "Portfolio of Alternative Assets: Why Not 100% Hedge Funds?" *Journal of Investing*, 8(4), pp. 87-97.

Lamm, Jr., R.M., and T. Ghaleb-Harter (2001) "Do Hedge Funds Belong in Taxable Portfolios?" *Journal of Wealth Management*, 4(1), pp. 58-73.

Lehmann, B.N., and D. Modest (1987) "Mutual Fund Performance Evaluation: A Comparison of Benchmarks and Benchmark Comparisons." *Journal of Finance*, 42, pp. 233-265.

Laporte Asset Allocation System / Zurich Capital Markets Database. http://www.laportesoft.com, Hackettstown, N.J.

Lavinio, S. (2000) *The Hedge Fund Handbook.* McGraw-Hill, New York.

Lawless, J.F. (1982) *Statistical Models and Methods for Lifetime Data.* John Wiley & Sons, New York.

Lederman, J., and R.A. Klein (1995) *Hedge Funds: Investment and Portfolio Strategies for the Institutional Investor*, Irwin Professional Publishing, New York.

Lee, C.F., and S. Rahman (1990) "New Evidence on Timing and Security Selection Skill of Mutual Fund Managers." *Journal of Portfolio Management*, 17, pp. 80-83.

Lehmann, B.N., and D. Modest (1987) "Mutual Fund Performance Evaluation: A Comparison of Benchmarks and Benchmark Comparisons." *Journal of Finance*, 42, pp. 233-265.

LHabitant, F.-S. (2002) "Assessing Market Risk for Hedge Funds and Hedge Fund Portfolios." *The Journal of Risk Finance*, 2(4), pp. 16-32.

Liang, B. (2000) "Hedge Funds: The Living and the Dead." *Journal of Financial and Quantitative Analysis*, 35(3), pp. 309-326.

Liang, B. (1999) "On the Performance of Hedge Funds." *Financial Analysts Journal*, 55, pp. 72-85.

Liew, J. (1999) *Essays in Investment Strategies*, UMI Dissertation Service, Ann Arbor, MI.

Litner, J. (1965) "The Valuation of Risk Assets and the Selection of Risky Investments in Stock Portfolios and Capital Budgets," *Review of Economics and Statistics*, 47, pp. 13-37.

London, D. (1987) *Survival Models and their Estimation.* ACTEX Publications, Winsted, CT.

MacKinnon, J.G. (1991) "Critical Values for Cointegration Tests in Long-Run Econometric Relationships." In Engle R.F. and C.W.J. Granger (Eds.) *Long-Run Economic Relationships: Readings in Cointegration.* Oxford University Press, New York.

Malkiel, B. (1998) *A Random Walk Down Wall Street.* Norton Publishers, New York.

Markowitz, H. (1991) *Portfolio Selection: Efficient Diversification of Investments.* Blackwell Publishers, UK.

Managed Accounts Report / Hedge (MAR/Hedge) (2001) October Newsletter, New York, http://www.marhedge.com.

McMullen, P., and R. Strong (1997) "Selection of Mutual Funds Using Data

Envelopment Analysis." *Journal of Business and Economic Studies*, 4, pp. 1-14.

Merton, R. (1981) "On Market Timing and Investment Performance Part I: An Equilibrium Theory of Value for Market Forecasts." *Journal of Business*, 54, pp. 363-406.

Michaud, R.O. (1998) *Efficient Asset Management: A Practical Guide to Stock Portfolio Optimization and Asset Allocation*. Harvard Business School Press, Boston, MA.

Michaud, R.O. (1989) "The Markowitz Optimization Enigma: Is Optimized Optimal?" *Financial Analysts Journal*, 45, pp. 31-42.

Miller, S.M., and A.G. Noulas (1996) "The Technical Efficiency of Large Bank Production." *Journal of Banking and Finance*, 20, pp. 495-509.

Morey, M.R., and R.C. Morey (1999) "Mutual Fund Performance Appraisals: A Multi-Horizon Perspective with Endogenous Benchmarking." *Omega*, 27, pp. 241-258.

Morley, I. (2001) "Alternative Investments: Perceptions and Reality." *Journal of Alternative Investments*, 3(4), pp. 62-64.

Murphy, J.A. (1986) "Futures Fund Performance: A Test Of The Effectiveness Of Technical Analysis." *Journal of Futures Markets*, 6(2), pp. 175-186.

Nawrocki, D. (1999) "A Brief History of Downside Risk Measures." *Journal of Investing*, 8(3), pp. 9-26.

Oral M., Kettani, O., and P. Lang (1991) "A Methodology for Collective Evaluation and Selection of Industrial R&D Projects." *Management Science*, 7 (37), pp. 871-885.

Park, J.M., and J.C. Staum (1998) "Fund of Funds Diversification: How Much is Enough?" *Journal of Alternative Investments*, 1(3), pp. 39-42.

Perron, P. (1988) "Trends and Random Walks in Macroeconomic Time Series," *Journal of Economic Dynamics and Control*, 12, pp. 297-332.

Peskin, M., Urias, M., Anjilvel, S., and B. Boudreau (2000) *Why Hedge Funds Makes Sense*. Quantitative Strategies, Morgan Stanley Dean Witter, New York.

Picerno, J. (2001) "The Happy World of Hedge Funds." *Bloomberg Wealth Manager*, New York, November 2001, pp. 64-72.

Pindyck, R.S., and D.L. Rubinfeld (1998) *Econometric Models and Economic Forecasts*, McGraw-Hill, New York.

President's Working Group on Financial Markets (1999) *Hedge Funds, Leverage, and the Lessons of Long-Term Capital Management*, Washington, DC.

Rao, R., and J.J. Szilagyi (1998) *The Coming Evolution of the Hedge Fund Industry: A Case for Growth and Restructuring*. KPMG Peat Marwick, New York.

Rennie, E.P., and T.J. Cowhey (1990) "The Successful Use of Benchmark Portfolios: A Case Study." *Financial Analysts Journal*, 46, pp. 18-26.

Roll, R. (1978) "Ambiguity When Performance is Measured by the Securities Line." *Journal of Finance*, 22, pp. 1051-1069.

Rostron, K., and B. Colvin (1999) "Multi-Manager Funds: A Manager's Perspective." *Journal of Alternative Investments*, 2(2), pp.56-62.

Schneeweis, T. (2001) "Hedge Funds: Risk and Return Alternatives for the Modern Investor", Presentation, June 2001, Center For International Securities and Derivatives Markets, University of Massachusetts.

Schneeweis, T. (1998) "Evidence of Superior Performance Persistence in Hedge Funds: An Empirical Comment." *Journal of Alternative Investments*, 1(2), pp. 76-79.

Schneeweis, T., and G. Georgiev (2002) "The Benefits of Managed Futures." CISDM Working Paper Series, University of Massachusetts.

Schneeweis, T., Kazemi, H., and G. Martin (2001) "Understanding Hedge Fund Performance: Research Results and Rules of Thumb of the Institutional Investors." CISDM Working Paper Series, University of Massachusetts.

Schneeweis, T., Savanayana, U. and D. McCarthy (1991) "Alternative Commodity Trading Vehicles: A Performance Analysis." *Journal of Futures Markets*, 11(6), pp.475-490.

Schneeweis, T., and R. Spurgin (2000) *Hedge Funds: Portfolio Risk Diversifiers, Risk Enhancers, or Both?* Isenberg School of Management, University of Massachusetts.

Schneeeweis T., and R. Spurgin (1999) "Alpha, Alpha, Who's Got the Alpha?" *Journal of Alternative Investments*, 2(3), pp. 83 - 87.

Schneeweis, T., and R. Spurgin (1998a) "Alternative Investments in Institutional Portfolios." CISDM Working Paper Series, University of Massachusetts.

Schneeweis, T., and R. Spurgin (1998b) "Multifactor Analysis of Hedge Funds, Managed Futures and Mutual Fund Return and Risk Characteristics." *Journal of Alternative Investments*, 1, pp. 1-24.

Schneeweis, T., Spurgin, R., and G. Georgiev (2001) "Benchmarking

Commodity Trading Advisor Performance with a Passive Futures-Based Index." CISDM Working Paper Series, University of Massachusetts.

Schneeweis, T., Spurgin, R., and D. McCarthy (1996) "Informational Content in Historical CTA Performance." CISDM Working Paper Series, University of Massachusetts.

Schneeweis, T., Spurgin, R., and M. Potter (1996) "Managed Futures and Hedge Fund Investments for Downside Equity Risk Management." *Derivatives Quarterly*, 3(1), pp. 62-72.

Sedzro, K., and D. Sardano (2000) "Mutual Fund Performance Evaluation Using Data Envelopment Analysis." In Chowdry B. (Ed.) *The Current State of Business*, Vol. 3, pp. 1125-1144, Spellbound Publications, India.

Sexton, T.R., Silkman, R.H., and A. Hogan (1986) "Data Envelopment Analysis: Critique and and Extensions." In Silkman, R.H. (Ed.) *Measuring Efficiency and Assessment of Data Envelopment Analysis*. Publication 32, New Directions of Program Evaluation, Jossey-Bass, San Francisco, CA.

Sharpe, M.J. (1999) "Constructing the Optimal Hedge Fund of Funds" *The Journal of Wealth Management*, 2(1), pp. 35-44.

Sharpe, W.F. (1964) "Capital Asset Prices: A Theory of Market Equilibrium Under Conditions of Risk," *Journal of Finance*, 19, pp. 425-442.

Sharpe, W.F. (1966) "Mutual Fund Performance." *Journal of Business*, 39(1), pp. 119-138.

Sharpe, W.F. (1992) "Asset Allocation: Management Style and Performance Measurement." *Journal of Portfolio Management*, 18(1), pp. 7-19.

Shefrin, H. (1999) *Beyond Greed and Fear: Understanding Behavioral Finance and the Psychology of Investing*. Harvard Business School Press, Cambridge, MA.

Sirri, E.R., and P. Tufano (1998) "Costly Search and Mutual Fund Flows." *Journal of Finance*, 53, pp. 1589-1622.

Solnik, B., and F. Longin (2001) "Extreme Correlation of International Equity Markets." *Journal of Finance*, 56(2), pp. 649-676.

Sortino, F., and R. van de Meer (1991) "Downside Risk." *Journal of Portfolio Management*, 17(4), pp. 27-31.

Spurgin, R. (1999) "A Study of Survival: Commodity Trading Advisors, 1988-1996." *Journal of Alternative Investments*, 2(3), pp. 16-22.

Stadlmann, M. (2001) "Hedge Funds and Absolute Returns." Westam Management, London, U.K.

Statman, M. (1987) "How Many Stocks make a Diversified Portfolio?" *Journal of Financial and Quantitative Analysis,* 22(3), pp.353-368.

TASS Investment Research (1999) *The Case for Hedge Funds.* Tremont Partners Inc., Rye, NY.

Temple, P. (2001) *Hedge Funds: Courtesans of Capitalism.* John Wiley & Sons, New York.

Thanassoulis, E., Boussofiane, A., and R.G. Dyson (1995) "Exploring Output Quality Targets in the Provisions of Perinatal Care in England Using Data Envelopment Analysis." *European Journal of Operational Research,* 80, pp. 588-607.

Tomlinson, B. (1998) *Why Standard Deviation is a Poor Measure of Risk.* Financial Risk Management Ltd., London, UK.

Treynor, J., and K. Mazuy (1966) "Can Mutual Funds Outguess the Market?" *Harvard Business Review,* 44, pp. 131-136.

Treynor, J. (1965) "How to Rate Management of Investment Funds." *Harvard Business Review,* 43(1), pp. 63-75.

Van Hedge (1999) "Number of Hedge Funds Increases for Tenth Consecutive Year." http://www.vanhedge.com.

Vassiloglou, M., and D. Giokas (1990) "A Study of Relative Efficiency of Bank Branches: An Application of Data Envelopment Analysis." *Journal of Operations Research Society,* 47, pp. 591-597.

White, H. (1980) "A Heteroskedasticity-Consistent Covariance Matrix Estimator and a Direct Test for Heteroskedasticity." *Econometrica,* 48(4), pp. 817-838.

White, J.B., and M.P. Miles (1999) "Last Year's Winners as This Year's Picks: An Analysis of Recent Hindsight as Mutual Fund Trading Rule?" *Journal of Financial and Strategic Decisions,* 12(1), pp. 69-72.

Zechner, J. (2000) "Performance Evaluation." Working Paper, University of Vienna.

Zurich Capital Markets (ZCM) / Laporte Asset Allocation System. http://www.laportesoft.com, Hackettstown, N.J.

Zhang, L. (1996) "Is Money Smart?" Working Paper, Yale School of Management.

INDEX

Page numbers followed by f indicate a figure
Page numbers followed by t indicate a table

Z

www.ingramcontent.com/pod-product-compliance
Ingram Content Group UK Ltd.
Pitfield, Milton Keynes, MK11 3LW, UK
UKHW040228290926
15471UKWH00001B/54

9 781587 98199